Forty Carats

A COMEDY IN TWO ACTS

Adapted by JAY ALLEN

From a play by

BARILLET and GREDY

SAMUEL FRENCH, INC.
25 WEST 45TH STREET   NEW YORK 10036
7623 SUNSET BOULEVARD   HOLLYWOOD 90046
80 RICHMOND ST. EAST   TORONTO, CANADA M5C 1P1
— *LONDON* —

FORTY CARATS, adapted by Jay Allen from a play by Barillet and Gredy, starring Julie Harris, directed by Abe Burrows, associate producer Samuel Leff, was presented by David Merrick at the Morosco Theatre, N.Y.C.

CAST OF CHARACTERS
(*In Order of Their Appearance*)

ANN STANLEY	*Julie Harris*
PETER LATHAM	*Marco St. John*
MRS. ADAMS	*Iva Withers*
MRS. MARGOLIN	*Polly Rowles*
BILLY BOYLAN	*Murray Hamilton*
EDDY EDWARDS	*Franklin Cover*
MAUD HAYES	*Glenda Farrell*
TRINA STANLEY	*Gretchen Corbett*
MRS. LATHAM	*Nancy Marchand*
MR. LATHAM	*John Cecil Holm*
PAT	*Michael Nouri*

The time is the present.

The play begins somewhere in the Greek Islands, then moves on to the office and the apartment of Ann Stanley in New York City.

Due authorship credit must be given on all programs, printing and advertising as follows:

Forty Carats

Adapted by Jay Allen

From a play by

Barillet and Gredy

The names of the authors shall appear in at least seventy-five percent (75%) of the size of the title type.

Forty Carats

ACT ONE

SCENE 1

(Prologue)

Before the Curtain rises, we hear a GREEK FOLK MELODY. This keeps going as the CURTAIN rises and continues for a bit under the opening action and dialogue.

The scene is the terrace of a little cafe in Greece. There are two crude wooden tables and some stools, sheltered against the burning sun by reed matting. In the background we see some of the Mediterranean and a Greek mountainside with some small white buildings on it. Upstage, leaning against one wall, there is a big, dusty American motorcycle. We actually see only part of it; the front wheel is Offstage. Standing behind the table Right is ANN STANLEY. She is wearing a wilted linen dress, sandals on her dusty feet. An overloaded native straw basket is beside her. A large straw hat is leaning against the basket. She is wiping her face and neck with a large handful of Kleenex. There are a lot of used tissues on the table in front of her. Also on the table is one shot glass. Speaking into a wall telephone near the doorway of the cafe Up Left is PETER LATHAM. He is a very young man, wearing khakis, shirt and sandals.

PETER. (*Into phone.*) Look, gyneka etho! Lady here. Gyneka etho!

5

ANN. (*Interrupts.*) *What?* What does he *say?*

PETER. (*Waving at her to be quiet.*) Gyneka etho . . . lady here . . . lady stranded! . . .

ANN. Lady hot . . . hot! (*She sits at table, takes Kleenex box from basket, puts it in her lap; takes out folding fan, begins to fan herself.*)

PETER. (*Into phone.*) Amaxi! . . . Amaxi! . . . Broken . . . Chevrolet spasmenos . . . Broken . . . What? . . . I don't understand . . . Pedi? . . . Oh, *pedi* . . . But . . . but . . . Okay . . . Okay . . . (*Discouraged.*) Esharisto. Thanks. (*Hangs up, comes over to her table shaking his head.*)

ANN. (*Gets up, puts fan in basket.*) What did they say? Will someone come?

(*MUSIC FADES OUT.*)

PETER. No chance. The mechanic's having a baby and there's no doctor.

ANN. (*Sits.*) A baby! What am I going to do about my car! How am I going to get back to Argos?

PETER. I've offered you a ride on my bike—

ANN. And I've told you I couldn't possibly ride on that thing.

PETER. Why not?

ANN. I am thirty-six years old!

PETER. Maybe if you tried sitting side-saddle. (ANN *gives him a look.*) Wait a minute. I know what you need. I'll be right back. (*He goes into cafe.* ANN *gets out a box of Baggies, tears one off, starts to fill it with the used Kleenexes. In a moment,* PETER *comes out with a bottle and a glass, puts them on her table, starts to pour.* ANN *puts a rubber band around the Baggie and replaces it in her basket.*) Now as soon as you're finished with that Kleenex commercial, this should help.

ANN. You do make yourself at home.

PETER. I come to this little joint all the time. I've been camped down on the beach for a couple of weeks.

ANN. Doing what?

PETER. Painting.

ANN. Are you an artist?

PETER. No.

ANN. A student?

PETER. No.

ANN. What are you, then?

PETER. What do *you* think I am?

ANN. I think you're a nutty kid, bumming around on a motorcycle.

PETER. (*Amiably.*) That's what I am. A nutty kid bumming around on a motorcycle.

ANN. (*Looks at drink.*) What's this?

PETER. Ouzo. Try it.

ANN. (*She reaches into her straw bag, takes out her own drinking glass, pours drink from glass on the table into her glass. Takes a sip, looks pleased.*) How old are you?

PETER. Twenty-two.

ANN. You don't look twenty-two.

PETER. You don't look thirty-six.

ANN. I don't look thirty-six because I'm thirty-eight. (*Sighs, empties glass.*) I took two years off for good behavior. (*Pours another drink.*) So just don't expect me to go roaring off cross-country on *that* thing. That . . . thing. (*With no warning,* ANN's *face puckers up and big tears begin to course down her cheeks.*)

PETER. (*Defensively, refers to motorcycle.*) That *thing* happens to be a Triumph Trophy Two-Fifty. (*Becomes aware of her tears.*) Hey, don't . . .

ANN. (*Puts down drink, rises, steps Down Right.*) What do you mean, hey, don't? I'm out here on a dead end road with no traffic, a broken-down car, and a pregnant mechanic. And it's so hot! I go off and leave my mother with a *fantastically* upset stomach. She's had it for four days and she didn't want to come to Greece in the first place.

PETER. You traveling with your mother?

ANN. (*Defensively.*) What's wrong with traveling with my mother? She's a charming woman and she's throwing up in that rotten little hotel . . . (*Sighs, squares her shoulders.*) Well, if I've got to spend the night here, I'd better see about getting a room.

PETER. A room? *Here?*

ANN. Well, a bed . . . in someone's house. (*He laughs.*) What's so funny?

PETER. (*Straightens his face.*) Nothing. Bugs aren't very funny.

ANN. Bugs? I shall sleep in the car.

PETER. I'll lend you my sleeping bag. You'll be more comfortable.

ANN. I'll be quite comfortable in the car.

PETER. No, you'll be quite miserable in the car.

ANN. Nevertheless. (*She picks up her bag.*) How much do I owe you?

PETER. What for?

ANN. My share of the drinks.

PETER. Thirteen cents. (*He crosses to her, holds out his hand. She realizes he is teasing her; her lip begins to tremble again. She sits in chair Right. He becomes alarmed.*) Don't start tearing up again . . . Look—will you just relax and let me handle this situation? If you're determined to wait here until the mechanic shows—which will certainly not be until tomorrow—you might as well be comfortable. Wait at my place.

ANN. What's your place?

PETER. I told you I have a sleeping bag.

ANN. Sleeping bag?

PETER. (*Points.*) Right down there.

ANN. Thank you, no.

PETER. Come on, hop on.

ANN. *No, thank you.*

PETER. You think I'm going to turn you back to mummy with "Hell's Angels" branded on your behind? Come on.

ANN. I am spending the night here . . . (ANN *turns furiously and marches toward the cafe door Left.*) Vo-ee-thai astynonia, epharisto psomi, apototos . . .

(PETER *listens to a moment of this open-mouthed.*)

PETER. What are you saying?

ANN. (*Furious with frustration.*) How do *I* know? I don't speak Greek. I want food! (*Speaks pitifully.*) I'm hungry. I have a very fast metabolism. (*Crosses to Down Center.*)

PETER. (*After a beat, crosses to her.*) Look, it'll take me about fifteen minutes to spear a fish—a nice big fish. It's what I do for dinner every night. I'll build a fire on the beach and grill the fish with some fennel. I've got some tomatoes and onions . . . We can go for a swim, then eat.

ANN. Swim. (*Turns to* PETER.) I don't have a suit.

PETER. (*Blandly.*) Neither do I.

(GREEK MUSIC STARTS.)

(*She looks at him for a moment, crosses up to table.* PETER *follows. She pours herself another drink, sips it. We should begin to suspect that she is just a little high.*)

ANN. (*Trying to remember.*) What did you call this drink?

PETER. Ouzo.

ANN. Ouzo. (*Drinks.*) It certainly is! (*She looks around.*) Oh, it's all so beautiful here. What's that smell? It's so sweet.

PETER. Myrtle. The whole island is covered with it. Myrtle is the flower sacred to Aphrodite.

ANN. (*Vaguely, dreamily.*) It is?

PETER. And the bay down there . . . Yithien . . . That's where Paris first made love to Helen after he carried her off.

ANN. Of Troy Helen?

PETER. (*Crosses two steps Left of table, turns, points another direction.*) I think they're supposed to have spent a night over there too—it's the same legend all over Greece . . . Hey, before we go swimming . . . what's your name?

ANN. (*A beat.*) Penelope.

PETER. (*Extending his hand.*) I'm Peter Latham.

ANN. Peter Latham.

(*They shake hands.*)

PETER. And what I'm offering here is a cool dip in the blue Aegean, a gourmet meal, civilized conversation—in *English* . . . (*Smiles charmingly.*) You'll forget your troubles.

ANN. Will I?

PETER. (*Crosses Up Left two steps.*) It's a promise. Come on.

ANN. (*A beat.*) Should I?

PETER. Sure.

ANN. (*Drinks.*) Really?

PETER. (*Gently, seriously.*) Yes, I really think you should.

ANN. (*Rises.*) Should we bring the bottle?

PETER. Great. Come on. (*He picks up bottle. She starts for the motorcycle, then stops.*)

ANN. Oh, dear . . .

PETER. (*Crosses to her.*) What's the matter?

ANN. I was just wondering how Helen of Troy managed about her mother.

BLACKOUT

(GREEK MUSIC)

ACT ONE

SCENE 2

A real estate office in the East Sixties. There is a desk Right, files Upstage, map of Manhattan Left. A door to ANN's private office Right, entrance door Left. On the walls are plans of apartments, photographs, etc.

On Stage is a woman, MRS. ADAMS, very well dressed, looking over a list and shaking her head.

MRS. ADAMS. No . . . no . . . no . . .

(MRS. MARGOLIN, *the office secretary, enters from the office door, Right. She is a motherly woman, sensible, good-natured, businesslike. She looks at* MRS. ADAMS, *then turns and speaks to* ANN, *who is not seen.*)

MRS. MARGOLIN. Mrs. Adams is still here.
ANN'S VOICE. (*Offstage.*) Please ask her to wait, Mrs. Margolin . . . I'll be with her in a few minutes.

(MRS. MAROGLIN *closes door and addresses* MRS. ADAMS.)

MRS. MARGOLIN. Mrs. Stanley is still busy. She is with a client.
MRS. ADAMS. I really *must* speak to her. There's nothing on this list. Nothing, nothing, nothing.
MRS. MARGOLIN. Mrs. Adams, that's the best list of apartments in New York.
MRS. ADAMS. These apartments are all impossible . . . There's one here that's not too bad, though. Ten-eighty Park Avenue. What is the cross street?
MRS. MARGOLIN. Eighty-eighth.
MRS. ADAMS. Eighty-eighth. (*Disappointed.*) It sounds perfect. But it's too far uptown—if you could give me this same apartment in the sixties . . .

MRS. MARGOLIN. We can't. It's attached to the building. (*PHONE rings. She sits as she answers it.*) Stanley Realty . . . Yes . . . Which one? . . . Oh, yes, of course! That's a marvelous apartment. And a lovely building—beautifully run. There's a closed-circuit television guarding all the elevators, closed-circuit television at the front door and at the back, and there are one-way see-through holes on both front and service doors of every apartment. They've put in newly-patented unpickable locks with chains, and it's a *lovely* neighborhood! . . . That *is* what you pay for, isn't it? . . . Well, *we* think the price is very reasonable . . . One hundred and sixty thousand, plus a maintenance of . . . Hello? Hello? (*Hangs up, mutters.*) That price is a real hangup.

(*A man comes in, not handsome but attractive and very sure of himself. He is smoking a cigar. He is* BILLY BOYLAN. *He seems quite at home as he crosses to* MRS. MARGOLIN.)

BILLY. Hi, there, Mrs. Margolin!

MRS. MARGOLIN. The actor's back.

BILLY. (*Pinches her cheek.*) The actor's back. Can I see Ann?

MRS. MARGOLIN. She's busy now. You'll have to wait. You know, she just got back from Greece.

BILLY. How was Greece? Did she have a good time?

MRS. MARGOLIN. Well, she went with her mother—

BILLY. You have answered my question.

(*He crosses to the bench Left, sits, smiles politely at* MRS. ADAMS, *opens a magazine and starts to read. He smokes his cigar.* MRS. ADAMS *watches him covertly, standing Left of* BILLY. MRS. MARGOLIN *busies herself with papers.*)

MRS. ADAMS. (*Finally to* BILLY.) Don't I know you?

BILLY. (*Pleasantly but without any encouragement whatever.*) I don't think so.

MRS. ADAMS. (*Persistent.*) Do you live in the neighbor-hood?

BILLY. No.

MRS. ADAMS. (*Sits by* BILLY *on bench.*) Are you sure we haven't met?

BILLY. (*A small smile.*) I'd remember. (*Back to maga-zine.*)

MRS. ADAMS. (*Takes this as a compliment.*) Oh . . . but I mean *really*, I could swear I've seen you . . .

BILLY. (*Shrugs.*) Movies . . . television . . .

MRS. ADAMS. (*Delighted.*) Oh, that's it! You're . . . you're—

BILLY. (*Cutting in wearily.*) Billy Boylan.

MRS. ADAMS. Of course. You're *Billy Boylan*.

BILLY. (*Nods.*) Billy Boylan.

MRS. ADAMS. Billy Boylan. (*She looks at him.*) Are you looking for an apartment? Mrs. Stanley has a lot of theatrical clients.

BILLY. (*Rises, crosses Right two steps.*) Yes, she has.

MRS. ADAMS. I'll bet she's a big fan of yours.

BILLY. (*He can take no more.*) I doubt it. I used to be her husband. (*Crosses up to file.*) Say, Margy—

MRS. ADAMS. Oh!

(ANN *comes out of the office carrying some papers.*)

ANN. Somebody left a blueprint out of this file.

MRS. MARGOLIN. *You* did.

ANN. (*Seeing* BILLY.) Hello, Billy. You're back.

(*They embrace.*)

BILLY. I'm back.

MRS. ADAMS. (*Rises, crosses to* ANN *and* BILLY.) Oh, Mrs. Stanley—

ANN. Oh, Mrs. Adams, I'm so sorry I've kept you waiting.

MRS. ADAMS. There's not a thing on this list that in-terests me.

ANN. Oh, for goodness sake, Mrs. Adams . . . (*Takes list from* MRS. ADAMS, *gives it to* MRS. MARGOLIN.) There's nothing on *that* list for Mrs. Adams.

MRS. MARGOLIN. Of course not!

ANN. (*Hands* MRS. ADAMS *her bag and gloves and begins to usher her toward door Left.*) Mrs. Adams, if you'll just give me a couple of days . . . well, make it next month, I have something coming in that I know you'll love.

MRS. ADAMS. (*Excited.*) What is it?

ANN. (*Going ahead of her to door Left, opens door.*) I can't say anything about it now.

MRS. ADAMS. Mrs. Stanley, if you can't trust *me*—

ANN. I really can't talk about it yet. (*Whispers.*) Big divorce coming up.

(*They embrace.*)

MRS. ADAMS. Oh, a divorce apartment. They're always the best! (*She goes.*)

ANN. (*Calling.*) Watch the columns, Mrs. Adams. (*She closes the door on the thoroughly satisfied* MRS. ADAMS. *She crosses to desk.*) She's a looker. Been looking through us for ten years. (*She takes blueprint from* MRS. MARGOLIN.) Have to see you later, Billy.

BILLY. Wait a minute. How was Greece?

ANN. It was covered with myrtle. (*She goes.*)

BILLY. (*To* MRS. MARGOLIN.) Myrtle . . . Hey, Margy, the trip seems to have done her good. (*He sits in chair in front of desk.*) What's she up to? Is she happy?

MRS. MARGOLIN. In her opinion, she's happy. In my opinion, she should have a husband.

BILLY. She's had two husbands.

MRS. MARGOLIN. Are we counting you?

BILLY. Certainly, we're counting me. She got a customer in there?

MRS. MARGOLIN. A rich one. Owns a string of hotels.

BILLY. Great. (*Pause.*) How's business generally?

MRS. MARGOLIN. You can't be broke again.

BILLY. There's no such word as "can't"!

MRS. MARGOLIN. But you've had three shows in the last month. I read where you go from New York and L.A., L.A. and New York . . .

BILLY. I stop off in between.

MRS. MARGOLIN. Las Vegas.

BILLY. Where else? Newark? Margy, I'm a lonely, rootless man.

ANN. (*Re-enters quickly.*) Margy, can you get me the keys for Eight-Eighty?

MRS. MARGOLIN. (*She gets up and heads for the file.*) Got him hungry?

ANN. Maybe.

BILLY. Annie! You're looking absolutely gorgeous. I've never seen you so goddam radiant!

ANN. You can't be broke again.

BILLY. I'm a lonely, rootless man. Just till the first, Annie.

MRS. MARGOLIN. (*Hands ANN the keys, crosses back to file.*) Here you go.

ANN. Thanks, Margy. (*Turns to go, then back to BILLY, waving the keys at him.*) If I put this one over, I'll help you out. How much do you need?

BILLY. I need a thousand. (ANN *starts for office door.*) But I'll take five hundred.

ANN. (*Turns back.*) Thanks. I need the money. (*She goes.*)

BILLY. (*Starting for door.*) 'Bye, Margy.

MRS. MARGOLIN. 'Bye. Mr. Boylan, you're a lonely, rootless son of a bitch.

BILLY. (*Turns back at door. Slightly reproving.*) Don't, Margy, that's what my mother used to call me. (*He goes.*)

(EDDY EDWARDS *enters from* ANN'S *office, followed by* ANN. *He is a big, well-set-up man in his forties. He crosses to Center.*)

ANN. Mrs. Margolin, Mr. Edwards has decided he's quite interested in Eight-Eighty. I'm going to take him over for a look.

EDDY. You wait here while I go whistle up that driver. He had to park around the block. We'll be out front in three minutes. (*Crosses Down Left.*)

MRS. MARGOLIN. Oh Lord, Eight-Eighty! (EDDY *stops and turns.*) I promised the Bigelows we'd hold off for at least another week on Eight-Eighty until they know whether their daughter—

EDDY. You got another buyer for the place? (*Turns to* ANN.) Look, Mrs. Stanley, you show me the layout and if I like it, you've got my check this afternoon.

ANN. I'll take it.

MRS. MARGOLIN. And I'll take care of the Bigelows.

EDDY. Thanks, Mrs. Margolin. I like your style. (*He starts off and turns again.*) You and I are going to get on just fine. What do you drink?

MRS. MARGOLIN. (*After a moment's thought.*) Diet-Pepsi?

EDDY. You'll get a case. (*He goes.*)

MRS. MARGOLIN. (*Crosses back to desk, grinning at* ANN.) A whole case!

ANN. (*Sits in chair in front of desk.*) I'm glad you reminded me about the Bigelows . . . *What* Bigelows! You made them up!

MRS. MARGOLIN. I lead a rich fantasy life. (*Looking at* ANN'S *shoes, clucks disapprovingly.*)

ANN. What's wrong?

MRS. MARGOLIN. Why don't you ever wear those cute red pumps?

ANN. I hate them. They hurt.

MRS. MARGOLIN. He's a bachelor. Limp a little.

ANN. Mr. Edwards?

MRS. MARGOLIN. He's rich. He makes quick decisions. Limp a little. (*Sits at desk.*)

ANN. Margy, will you get it through your head that I am no longer a Venus flytrap. I am thirty-eight years old —going on thirty-nine.

MRS. MARGOLIN. (*Hands over ears.*) I didn't hear it! I refuse to hear it!

ANN. You heard it. For the thousandth time, I am a middle-aged woman with a seventeen-year-old daughter. (*Rises, starts for door.*)

(*PHONE rings.*)

MRS. MARGOLIN. (*Picks up phone.*) Stanley Realty ...

ANN. See you tomorrow, Margy.

MRS. MARGOLIN. (*Into phone.*) Will you hold it a minute, please? (*To* ANN.) You call thirty-eight middle-aged!

ANN. Sure.

MRS. MARGOLIN. Well! I have never been so insulted in my life.

ANN. Give up, Margy. We've all gotta go sometime. (*She goes.*)

MRS. MARGOLIN. (*Into phone.*) Sorry to keep you waiting ... Yes, we handle suburban rentals. Could you give me some idea of the price you had in mind? ... About a hundred and fifty a month ... *Where?* ... In Greenwich. Well, I really don't think you're going to find anything in Greenwich for that price ... Now look, dear, would you be willing to go a little further out of town? ... Well, like Cleveland.

BLACKOUT

ACT ONE

SCENE 3

Living room of ANN's *apartment.*

It is almost six in the evening. Very loud rock MUSIC [the same heard in the scene change] is heard over the radio. On rise, MAUD, Ann's mother, is sitting,

legs outstretched on the divan, reading a magazine.
She wears a simple smart dress suitable to her age.
But on her legs are bright red stockings. She is also
wearing large pearl earrings. After a moment, TRINA,
her granddaughter, enters from the hall.

TRINA. Granny, have you seen my big pearl earrings?

MAUD. No, dear, I haven't. (TRINA *moves first to the*
desk, then to the bar, spots the earrings on MAUD'S *ears,*
crosses, turns off the RADIO. She goes to MAUD *and takes*
off the earrings.) I didn't realize I had them on.

TRINA. (*Having retrieved the earrings, she has begun*
to sniff suspiciously. Behind sofa.) What's that? That
perfume?

MAUD. Hmm?

TRINA. That's my Jolie Madame.

MAUD. Oh, I didn't realize I had that on.

TRINA. Granny, will you please stay the hell out of my
Jolie Madame?

MAUD. (*Quickly taking the offensive.*) Why do you
wear your hair like that? It ruins your profile.

TRINA. (*Suddenly looks at* MAUD'S *tights.*) Those
tights. Those red tights!

MAUD. What red tights?

TRINA. (*Attempts to pull up* MAUD'S *skirt and* MAUD
fights back.) Those are my red tights, and don't tell me
you didn't realize you had them on.

MAUD. Oh, I realized I had them on. I just didn't
realize they were red.

TRINA. Look, Granny, I don't mess around in your
Supp-Hose.

MAUD. Trina, what time did you come in last night?

TRINA. (*Crossing to mirror and putting on earrings.*)
Around five.

MAUD. Five a.m.?

TRINA. Five a.m.

MAUD. You haven't even the decency to lie. Who were
you out with till five a.m.?

TRINA. Mark and Rudy and Bert.

MAUD. Mark *who?* Rudy *who?* Bert *who?*

TRINA. (*Turns back to* MAUD, *shrugs.*) Who goes formal? They're just kids I go dancing with or shoot a little pool.

MAUD. Shoot a little pool! How feminine!

(*The DOORBELL rings.*)

TRINA. (*Starts for door.*) It's Arthur for me.

MAUD. (*Assumes sitting position on sofa.*) Arthur? You've never mentioned an Arthur. Arthur who?

TRINA. I'll ask him when he comes in. (TRINA *opens the door.*)

(*We see the young man. He is the same one we met in the Prologue,* PETER LATHAM. *He is now wearing a turtleneck sweater and is carrying a sports jacket.*)

PETER. (*Confidently entering.*) Hello. Are you Trina Stanley?

TRINA. Who are you?

MAUD. He's *Arthur.*

PETER. Peter.

MAUD. Arthur Peter. All right.

PETER. Didn't Arthur call? (TRINA *shakes her head.*) Oh, well, since he lives right around the block from my date and I'm over here by you, we exchanged. (*Sees the blank look.*) I mean, I'm picking you up for Arthur and he's bringing my date.

TRINA. (*Accepts this. They start to go.*) Okay.

MAUD. (*Sharply.*) Trina, if you don't mind. I'd like to meet Arthur.

TRINA. (*Closes door, brings* PETER *down Right. She crosses Upstage sofa.*) This isn't Arthur. This is Peter. My grandmother, Mrs. Hayes.

MAUD. How do you do? (*As they shake hands,* PETER *helps* MAUD *to her feet.*) Thank you. And where are you delivering my granddaughter this evening?

TRINA. (*Impatiently. Crosses Down Left.*) 'Night,
Granny Maud.

MAUD. (*Crosses Down two steps.*) But I wish to know
where "Peter" is taking you, Trina.

PETER. We're going to meet Arthur and the others at
the Electric Circus.

MAUD. (*Crosses Left to* TRINA.) Then on to some pool
emporium, I presume?

TRINA. (*Her voice rising.*) You'll pay for this, Granny!

MAUD. I simply want to know where you're—

TRINA. I'll tell you what, Granny, take off my tights.
Right now!

(PETER *drifts Down Right.* ANN *enters from bedroom,
wearing robe and slippers and carrying a bottle of
Vitabath and a towel.*)

MAUD. You are not leaving this house with a boy whose
last name you don't even know.

ANN. My Vitabath's all gone! Who's been—? (*Crosses
to* TRINA *and* MAUD. *Suddenly stops, turns, as she realizes*
PETER *is standing there.*)

TRINA. Granny did it.

MAUD. (*Facing* TRINA.) Ann, this young man, whom
Trina has never met, nor, I gather, even heard of, rings
the doorbell as a proxy for Arthur—

TRINA. He had the decency to pick me up as a *favor*
to Arthur!

(*Throughout the above exchange,* ANN *casts stunned
glances at* PETER. PETER *looks amazed and then
pleased.*)

MAUD. Arthur *who?*

TRINA. (*Shouting.*) How do *I* know! He's a friend of
Peter's!

MAUD. Peter *who?*

PETER. Peter Latham.

TRINA. (*Triumphantly.*) Peter *Latham!*

MAUD. Peter Latham. All right! (*Thoughtfully.*) Latham . . . I went to school with a Latham girl. From Pittsburgh. Isabella Latham.

PETER. She's my aunt.

MAUD. (*Absolutely delighted, turns toward* PETER.) *No!* Isn't that extraordinary! If Isabella is your aunt, then you're a Hohenhauser.

PETER. My mother was a Hohenhauser.

MAUD. What a teeny-weeny world! (*She starts toward* PETER, *pushing* ANN *ahead of her.*) Well! Ann, this is Peter Latham. This is Trina's mother, Mrs. Stanley.

ANN. How do you do?

PETER. How do you do, Mrs. Stanley?

MAUD. Trina, please ask Mr. Latham to sit down.

ANN. No! Mother, he doesn't want to sit down. Can't you see they want to go along? Have a nice evening, Trina. Don't . . . stay out too late. (*Kisses* TRINA, *pushes her towards the door. To* PETER.) Good night . . . uh . . .

PETER. (*Starting to go.*) Peter.

ANN. Good night, Peter.

MAUD. (*Following* PETER.) Good night, children. Have fun.

PETER. Good night, Mrs. Stanley.

TRINA. (*At door with* PETER.) Good night, Mummy. Good night, Granny Maud . . . (*Shakes her head.*) you really are something else! Come on, Pete. (*They exit.*)

MAUD. A Hohenhauser! Ann, a *Hohenhauser!* (*Crosses Down Right, sits on arm of sofa.*)

ANN. (*Crosses Upstage Right to bar, shakily begins to fix herself a drink.*) Tell me about the Hohenhausers. They're in steel, aren't they?

MAUD. Ann, dear, the Hohenhausers are in *money.*

ANN. And the . . . Lathams? (*Slugs down drink, pours herself another.*)

MAUD. (*Eagerly.*) Well . . . Isabella Latham had, I think it was two brothers. Or was it three? Oh well, *that* doesn't matter. What matters is that this one brother married the Hohenhauser girl who must have inherited *everything* . . . and this boy . . . this *Peter*, is the *son*. Didn't you think he was absolutely charming? How old do you think he is? About twenty?

ANN. (*Slugs down another drink, speaks quite definitely.*) Twenty-two.

BLACKOUT

(*ROCK 'N' ROLL MUSIC*)

ACT ONE

SCENE 4

Late afternoon, two days later.

ANN'S *office.* MRS. MARGOLIN *is typing.* ANN *enters from her own office. Puts her purse on the file.*

ANN. It's after five. Why don't you go on home?

MRS. MARGOLIN. I'm just finishing up this lease . . . (*As she rises, the PHONE rings. She picks it up.*) Stanley Realty . . . Who's calling? (*Lifts her eyebrows, pleased.*) Oh, Mr. Edwards. . . . Mrs. Stanley is right here. Just a moment. (*Hands phone to* ANN.)

ANN. Hello, Eddy, I was just about to leave . . . Oh . . . Well, dinner sounds fine . . . No, no, I'd really rather go home first and get myself pulled together . . . Oh, give me about an hour and a half . . . Fine. See you then . . . Oh, it's apartment eight-B. B as in . . .

MRS. MARGOLIN. Bouillabaisse.

ANN. Bouillabaisse . . . Okay? . . . 'Bye. (*She hangs up.*)

(*During the above,* MRS. MARGOLIN *has been standing*

*near the desk, listening to the conversation with great
interest.*)

MRS. MARGOLIN. You must have limped real good.
(*Crosses to coat rack, starts to get into her coat.*)
ANN. I'm helping Mr. Edwards with the decorating.
Just the basic colors.
MRS. MARGOLIN. Good. Keep the whole business basic.
ANN. Margy, I'm not interested in Mr. Edwards.

(*At this moment, the outer door opens and* PETER, *in
well-tailored slacks and jacket, enters.* ANN *freezes.*
MRS. MARGOLIN *sees her look, turns and sees* PETER.
He is very cool, very in control.)

PETER. (*Crosses to Center.*) Hello, I'm glad I caught
you in.
ANN. (*Moving Right, away from him.*) Good after-
noon, Mr. Latham. I was just leaving.
PETER. I'll take you home.
ANN. (*Conscious of* MRS. MARGOLIN'S *curious gaze.*)
No, thank you, I'm . . . (*To* MRS. MARGOLIN.) This is
Mr. Latham. Mr. Latham is . . . is . . .
PETER. (*Helps* MRS. MARGOLIN *with her coat.*) Look-
ing for a studio apartment.
ANN. (*Sits at desk.*) Yes. That's right. I'll take care of
it, Mrs. Margolin. You go along.
MRS. MARGOLIN. I see. (*Takes her bag, goes to door
Left.*) Don't forget you've got an appointment tonight.
With Mr. Edwards.
ANN. I won't forget.
MRS. MARGOLIN. I see. (*She goes.*)

(*There is a moment of silence.*)

PETER. (*Crosses to desk.*) Penelope. Penelope Schwartz.
(ANN *smiles, gives a small shrug.*) That's a pretty strong
defense. Give a guy the wrong name and number so that

when he doesn't call, it's because he couldn't, not because he didn't want to.

ANN. Did you really try to find Miss Schwartz? It never occurred to me that you would.

PETER. Why did you cut out? The next morning you disappeared. You just cut out.

ANN. I'm sorry. But now you see why. I mean, among other things, I am the mother of a grown daughter.

PETER. Let's have dinner.

ANN. Peter, you're very sweet, but I can't have dinner with you. I can't see you again.

PETER. Look, there's no button on my lapel—"STANLEY REALTY SLEEPS AROUND."

ANN. (*Rises, crosses Down Right.*) Now please listen to me. This entire situation is . . . is just horribly embarrassing.

PETER. Let's have dinner.

ANN. (*Turns to him.*) Peter. I can't be seen running around with a . . . (*Smiles ruefully.*) You're just a kid. I could be arrested.

PETER. (*Grins.*) Risk it.

ANN. (*Crosses back to desk.*) You've got to understand my position.

PETER. I do. I understand your position.

ANN. Then you must realize why I can't see you again. I'm sorry, but that's the way it is.

PETER. I see.

ANN. I'm really sorry.

PETER. I'm sorry, too.

ANN. Thank you, Peter. You're very understanding. (*Holds out her hand.*) Goodbye, Peter.

(PETER *takes her hand.* MAUD *enters in a flurry with umbrella and raincoat.* ANN *takes her hand away.*)

MAUD. It's a cloudburst! I was on my way from— (*Sees* PETER, *lights up.*) Why, Peter Latham! How nice to see you.

(*He crosses to her, they shake hands.*)

PETER. Hello, Mrs. Hayes. That's a very dashing raincoat.

MAUD. I'm *so* glad you like it. It's Trina's . . . What are you doing here?

ANN. Mr. Latham is—

PETER. I'm looking for an apartment.

ANN. Yes.

PETER. I thought Mrs. Stanley might be able to help me.

ANN. Unfortunately, I haven't *a thing to offer him.*

MAUD. (*Very cordial.*) But how nice of you to come to Ann.

PETER. Natural selection.

MAUD. That's sweet.

ANN. H'mmm.

MAUD. (*Crosses to desk.*) I've been to the hairdresser. Rain! Wouldn't you know? Naturally, not a taxi in sight. I guess we'll just have to sit it out. (*Sits in chair in front of desk.*)

ANN. Mother, I can't wait. I have a date and I have to change. So let's make a dash for the subway.

MAUD. The subway!

PETER. I have my car here.

MAUD. (*Adoringly.*) Aren't you marvelous!

ANN. (*Crosses to file, picks up bag. To PETER.*) Absolutely marvelous. But I don't want to take you out of your way—

MAUD. (*Cutting in firmly.*) Now I'm sure Mr. Latham—

PETER. Peter.

MAUD. (*Smiling cozily.*) Peter . . . wouldn't mind dropping us off. Especially if we ask him up for tea.

PETER. Why, I'd love to.

ANN. (*Cutting in sharply.*) Mother, I told you I—

MAUD. (*Airily rises, goes to PETER, takes his right arm.*) Oh, yes, you have a date. Well, then, Trina and I

will have to look after Peter. (*To* PETER.) Trina will be
delighted to see you.

(ANN *sits dejectedly in chair in front of desk.*)

PETER. I'm sure she will. I owe her seventeen dollars.
She hustled me in a poolroom. Well . . . my car's parked
right outside. (*He takes* MAUD *to the door. She picks up
her umbrella.*) It's the little red Maserati.

MAUD. A Maserati . . . Ah, la dolce vita! (*She goes.*)

PETER. (*Crosses to coat rack, gets her coat and scarf.*)
Come on. Let's go.

ANN. (*Rises.*) Peter, I do not want you to come up to
my apartment.

PETER. I promised your mother.

ANN. This is ridiculous, Peter, and I . . .

PETER. (*He begins to bundle her into her coat.*) Left.
Your *left* arm . . . (ANN *is forced to change her purse
from the left hand to the right.*) That's a girl . . .

ANN. You cannot behave like this!

PETER. Do you really have a date tonight?

ANN. Yes, I do.

(*He starts buttoning her up, does so incorrectly. She pulls
away from him, begins fumbling with the buttons.*)

PETER. Who have you got a date with?

ANN. Please! I can button my own coat!

(*She crosses toward door.* PETER *follows.*)

PETER. Who have you got a date with?

ANN. (*Stops, turns to him.*) Now, Peter, we're going
out to the car. And you're going to drive Mother and me
home. Then you're going to say you just remembered an
appointment you forgot, and you're going to excuse yourself. You will then say goodbye and drive away into the

sunset in your little red Maserati. You will definitely not come up. You are not to telephone me, you are not to come to this office again, and— (*She goes through the door, but her VOICE goes on.*) you will never again come to my apartment . . .

PETER. (*As he goes.*) We'll talk about it up at your place.

BLACKOUT

(*ROCK 'N' ROLL MUSIC*)

ACT ONE

SCENE 5

ANN's *apartment. A little later.*

PETER *is sitting in desk chair. He rises, reaches for ouzo bottle on bar, looks at it.* TRINA *enters from hall. He puts down bottle.*

TRINA. Hi! What brought you?

PETER. I just happened to meet your grandmother and she invited me up.

TRINA. Oh.

(MAUD *enters from kitchen.*)

PETER. Mrs. Hayes, I see you've got some ouzo.

MAUD. That's a ghastly drink.

TRINA. (*To* PETER.) Mummy's been hooked on it ever since she and Granny got back from Greece.

PETER. (*Pleased.*) Oh.

MAUD. (*Hates the thought of Greece.*) Do you know Greece?

PETER. A little.

TRINA. Granny hated it.

MAUD. I couldn't bear the food. All that oil.

PETER. I know. It can give you a fantastically upset stomach.

MAUD. Exactly! Well, I must make a phone call. (*Crosses to* TRINA.) I'm sure you young people can get along without me for a moment. You two must have a lot to talk about. (*She pushes* TRINA *towards* PETER *and goes.*)

TRINA. (*After a beat.*) You owe me— (*Puts out hand.*)

PETER. (*Brings money from pocket.*) Seventeen bucks. I have it ready. (*Hands her the money.*)

TRINA. (*Counts it, slips it into her boot.*) Poor concentration. That's your trouble. (*Slouches on sofa.*)

PETER. (*Slouches in chair Right.*) M'mmm. Pretty wet out there today.

TRINA. Yeah. All day.

PETER. I don't mind rain.

TRINA. Rain's okay.

PETER. So, what's new since the other night?

TRINA. Nothing much. What's new with you?

PETER. Nothing. (*Rising.*) It's great talking to you.

TRINA. You too.

PETER. Say, where'd you learn to shoot pool like that?

TRINA. My step-father.

PETER. H'mmm. *Who?*

TRINA. Mummy's second husband.

PETER. Oh.

MAUD. (*Entering from hall.*) I just told them they'd have to play without me tonight. I am *not* going out in this weather. (*To* TRINA.) Trina, did you know your mother's finding an apartment for Peter?

TRINA. Oh?

MAUD. Well, Peter, will you be living permanently in New York? One always associates your family with Pittsburgh.

TRINA. Pittsburgh. Eachh.

MAUD. (*Crosses up behind* TRINA.) Trina, dear, you've absolutely no experience with the rich cultural life of regional America. People live very pleasantly indeed outside of New York.

TRINA. In *Pittsburgh?* You couldn't pay me.

MAUD. (*Trying to shut her up.*) Pittsburgh's lovely. (*To* PETER.) If I'm not mistaken . . . your grandparents had that extraordinary house just outside of Pittsburgh . . . What was it called?

PETER. "Belwood."

MAUD. "Belwood"!

PETER. My parents live there now. The Hohenhauser Astrodome.

TRINA. If you're so rich, you ought to make Mummy get you one of those sexy apartments at River House.

MAUD. Trina, I'm sure Peter has told your mother exactly what he wants.

PETER. Exactly. (*Looks at watch.*) I wanted to talk it over with her. How long do you think she'll be?

TRINA. (*With a shrug.*) She's getting dressed.

MAUD. Trina, do you know who Ann's having dinner with this evening? She's being very mysterious.

TRINA. What's she got to be mysterious about?

MAUD. A beau?

TRINA. Oh, come off it.

PETER. Why do you say that?

TRINA. You don't know my mother. Actually . . . (*Turns her attention directly to* PETER.) I mean, you don't have to be diplomatic, but wouldn't you honestly say she was still pretty attractive? I mean for her age?

PETER. Yes, I would.

TRINA. I mean if you were an older man, *you'd* find her attractive.

PETER. (*Judiciously.*) I believe I would. Yes.

TRINA. Well, she wouldn't find *you* attractive.

MAUD. (*Crosses Up Left of sofa.*) Trina! How can you be so rude!

TRINA. Oh, Granny Maud, I'm just trying to say that Mummy doesn't find *anybody* attractive. She *refuses* to find anybody attractive. Two divorces and she's out of business.

MAUD. Trina, I don't think Peter is interested in—
(*Crosses Down Left of sofa, sits.*)

TRINA. Actually, Mummy is very naive about men and she's been sort of burned.

PETER. I see.

TRINA. So she just *doesn't*. If you know what I mean.

MAUD. (*Laughs as though it was a joke.*) Trina! (ANN *enters from the bedroom, wearing a short dinner dress. She looks very glamorous. Both* TRINA *and* MAUD *are impressed and somewhat mystified.* ANN *crosses to coffee table, picks up a cigarette.*) Well . . . That's *new*.

TRINA. Not bad.

ANN. (*Quite pleased with herself.*) Do you like it?

MAUD. It's lovely!

TRINA. It's really okay! Peter, tell her it's okay.

PETER. It's okay!

MAUD. Isn't it a little too short?

PETER. *No!* (*All* THREE WOMEN *turn to stare at him. He is embarrassed.*) I mean . . . it looks perfect. To *me*. It really does. *Perfect*.

(*He crosses to* ANN *at Left a bit too quickly, lights her cigarette. She turns away, he counters Upstage.*)

MAUD. My goodness, who's all this for?

TRINA. Who rates the parade?

ANN. Well, really! Must you two act as if I spend all my evenings schlumping around in snowshoes!

MAUD. Well, you're obviously out to overwhelm somebody! Who?

ANN. I have a *business* date with a Mr. Edwards. (*Stubs out cigarette in ashtray by sofa.* PETER *starts to cross Right Upstage of sofa. She starts Right towards end table by chair.*) What time is it?

PETER. Six forty-five.

MAUD. Don't be nervous.

ANN. I am not at all nervous! (*She takes another cigarette.*)

MAUD. You know how traffic is.

(*Again* PETER *moves swiftly in to light it. He startles her. She yelps.*)

ANN. Stop creeping up on me!

(*The DOORBELL rings.*)

TRINA. (*Starts for door.*) Shall I go?

ANN. *I'll* go. (TRINA *stops.* ANN *starts toward the door.* MAUD, TRINA *and* PETER *stare in fascination.* ANN, *at door, turns, sees them.*) What is the matter with you? Will you please relax? (MAUD *and* TRINA *sit on sofa Left,* PETER *follows, sits on sofa Right.* EACH *tries to think of something to say.*) Talk among yourselves. (ANN *opens the door.* EDDY EDWARDS *appears.*)

MAUD. I had the craziest poker game Thursday night. There was Mrs. Peterson, Mrs. Tillit and Mrs. Bayard . . . Cynthia Bayard . . .

ANN. (*To* EDDY.) Hello.

EDDY. (*Taking in* ANN's *appearance.*) Wow! (*The* THREE PEOPLE *stop speaking when they hear* EDDY *and turn to look at him.*) When you pull yourself together you really get everything in the right place! (*He looks at the* THREE *on the sofa.*)

ANN. (*A small nervous laugh.*) Come in . . . come in . . . (*Closes door.*)

EDDY. (*Crossing Down Right on sofa, looking around apartment.*) Very nice. You really have the touch, lady. (*Looks at* TRIO *on sofa.*) Say, I . . .

ANN. (*Crosses to* EDDY's *Right.*) I'm afraid we're . . . (PETER, TRINA *and* MAUD *rise.*) It's a bit of a family evening, Mr. Edwards—

EDDY. (*Delighted.*) I like that!

ANN. Mother, may I present Mr. Edwards . . . My mother, Mrs. Hayes.

MAUD. My daughter has talked so much about you, Mr. Edwards.

EDDY. (*Pleased.*) Is that a fact?

ANN. And this is my daughter, Trina . . .

TRINA. How do you do, Mr. Edwards?

EDDY. Hello, young lady . . . Looks seem to run in the family . . . (*Turns to* PETER.) And this is your son.

ANN. What?

EDDY. Hi there, fella! (*Waves genially.*)

PETER. (*Imitating wave.*) I'm Peter Latham.

MAUD. Peter is a friend of my granddaughter's, Mr. Edwards.

EDDY. Natural mistake. (*To* ANN.) He's handsome enough to be yours.

ANN. (*Drily.*) Thank you. Something to drink, Eddy?

EDDY. (*Sits in chair Right.*) Bourbon . . . rocks . . . no water. (ANN *motions for the* THREE *to sit, then crosses to bar and starts mixing the drink.*) It's great to be around a family together like this . . . my wife died a year ago.

ANN. I'm so sorry. I didn't know.

MAUD. My daughter tells me you've just acquired a marvelous new apartment.

TRINA. And very expensive. I hear Mummy clipped you.

(ANN *crosses to* EDDY, *gives him the drink.*)

EDDY. (*Laughs.*) That's right, kid. And I loved it. A dinky little apartment and this pretty little lady looks you straight in the eye and says a hundred and fifty, and you know she means big ones.

ANN. That's high-class clipping.

EDDY. Say, I hope you will throw in some free advice. You could give me a couple of hints about drapes and chintz and all that shit . . . (*Realizes what he has said, looks very embarrassed.*)

ANN. (*Crosses Down Right to bedroom door. Drily.*) I never heard the decorating business more accurately described.

(*She goes.* EDDY *gulps down his drink.*)

MAUD. (*Social manner.*) Has the rain let up, Mr. Edwards?

EDDY. (*Gratefully.*) A bit.

MAUD. You stay, Peter. You can join us for a *petit diner.*

(PETER *smiles, looks at* TRINA, *hesitates.*)

PETER. Well . . .

TRINA. It's okay, Pete. You can stay if you want. (*Puts legs up on coffee table.*)

PETER. Thanks, I'd like to.

TRINA. And later we can shoot some pool at McGirr's.

EDDY. (*With interest.*) A little girl like you shooting pool?

PETER. (*To* EDDY.) She just *looks* like a girl. She's really Paul Newman.

(ANN *returns carrying a purse and gloves.*)

ANN. I'm ready.

EDDY. (*On his feet.*) Then I guess we're off. But I sure hate to leave all these nice people . . .

ANN. (*Looking at them.*) Well, *I* don't. (*Crosses to sofa.*) Good night, Mother . . . Trina. *Goodbye,* Peter.

PETER. I'll probably be here when you get back. (*Puts legs up on coffee table.*)

MAUD. Trina, take your feet off the table.

ANN. (*To* PETER.) You, too.

(*They comply.* ANN *goes towards the door.*)

EDDY. Mrs. Hayes, it's been good talking to you. Good night, young lady. So long, son. (*Points index finger at* PETER. PETER *imitates.*)

PETER. Sir.

(ANN *opens the door, disclosing* BILLY *on the threshold, a bag of Chinese food in cartons in his arms.*)

BILLY. I was just about to ring. I'm not too late?

ANN. About eight years.

BILLY. You invited me to dinner.

ANN. I said call me Wednesday and if it's convenient we can have dinner together.

BILLY. This is outrageous! I brought moo goo gai pan. You *love* moo goo gai pan. (*Shoves bag into her hand.*)

EDDY. Uh . . . Mrs. Stanley . . . if you really had a date with your beau—

ANN. He's not my beau, and I did *not* have a date with him. He's just a . . . part-time ex-husband.

EDDY. (*Puzzled.*) Oh.

BILLY. (*Goes to* EDDY, *near bar, hand outstretched.*) Billy Boylan.

EDDY. Eddy Edwards. (*Instantly recognizing the name, then the face, begins to beam. He takes the proffered hand, shakes it enthusiatically.*) *Billy Boylan.* I've seen you on "Peyton Place"! (*To* ANN.) Billy Boylan!

ANN. (*Wearily.*) Billy Boylan. (*To* EDDY.) Eddy, let's go.

BILLY. (*To* ANN.) You're seriously going to dump me tonight?

MAUD. (*Gets up, takes bag from* ANN.) If you're feeling abandoned, Billy, you can stay with us. *We'll* eat your moo goo gai pan. (*Starts for kitchen, stops.*)

EDDY. Listen . . . you know it just seems like a shame to go off and leave a party.

ANN. (*Protesting sincerely.*) Oh, please!

EDDY. (*Crosses to* ANN *at door.*) I've got an idea . . . I'll get the driver to hurry over to the Caviarteria . . . caviar . . . smoked turkey . . . salmon . . .

MAUD. Be sure it's fresh caviar.

EDDY. Sure!

BILLY. Wine! We'll need wine.

EDDY. Right! We'll have a real party. Right *here!* Okay? Okay?

BILLY. Marvy!

MAUD. Lovely!

ANN. (*She stands frustrated, unable to get a word in.*) Swell!

EDDY. I'll be right back! (*He stops, turns with a broad, happy smile.*) Billy Boylan! (*He goes.*)

BILLY. (*Crosses to* MAUD *Upstage of sofa.*) What a darling guy.

(PETER *gets up.*)

TRINA. He's nice.

MAUD. And very *generous.*

ANN. (*Crossing Down Right, to* PETER.) I hope *you* like him. (*She motions for him to sit again. She goes furiously into bedroom to put away her purse and gloves.*)

BILLY. Hey there, Granny Maud, we'll do the table.

MAUD. (*As she goes for the kitchen.*) Salmon and caviar. I'll get the pink plates. (*She goes.*)

(PETER *rises.*)

TRINA. (*Heading for her room.*) I'm going to change. (*She goes.*)

BILLY. (*Who has started for the kitchen, now notices* PETER, *turns back.*) You're . . .

PETER. Peter Latham.

ANN. (*Entering from bedroom.*) Trina's friend.

BILLY. Hello, Peter. Billy Boylan.

(*They shake hands.*)

PETER. Billy Boylan.

BILLY. (*Crossing towards kitchen.*) Well, let's get this show on the road. (*Turns back.*) Glad to have you aboard, Pete.

PETER. Thanks. (BILLY *exits, leaving* ANN *and* PETER *alone for a moment. She starts towards the kitchen.*) How about you, Ann?

ANN. What about me?

PETER. (*Goes to her.*) Are *you* glad to have me aboard?

ANN. (*Stops.*) What?

PETER. Are *you* glad to have me aboard? (*He kisses her, she starts to respond. Suddenly pushes him away, looks at him thoughtfully.*) Answer me!

ANN. What was the question?

BLACKOUT

(*FAST GYPSY MUSIC*)

ACT ONE

SCENE 6

ANN'S *apartment, the next day. Sunday afternoon, about five o'clock.*

A television set is on. We hear the sound of a BAND at half time. BILLY's jacket is on chair Right. On the sofa in his shirtsleeves and wearing an apron lies BILLY, sound asleep. The TV set is on his stomach. TRINA comes out of her room dressed to go out. She imitates a drum majorette with a baton.

TRINA. Hey, Billy, tell Mummy I've gone.

(BILLY *does not waken.* TRINA *shuts off TV, puts it on end table Left of sofa.* BILLY *wakes up, startled.*)

BILLY. Don't do that! I'm watching the game.

TRINA. It's half-time. You were sleeping.

BILLY. Resting. That damned party last night.

TRINA. You look very sweet in that apron.

BILLY. (*Gets into sitting position.*) Pucci. Ann lured me into this by saying, "Come on over and finish up the caviar."

TRINA. (*Proudly.*) I finished it this morning.

BILLY. I noticed. What Ann meant was, "Come on over and finish the dishes."

TRINA. 'Bye.

(ANN *enters from kitchen, carrying a tray with ice bucket, liquor, etc.*)

ANN. (*To* BILLY.) The dishes are done. (*Crosses Upstage sofa to bar. To* TRINA.) Where are you off to?

TRINA. To the flicks with some kids. 'Bye, Billy. You were absolutely dazzling last night. The competition from Eddy must have stimulated you.

(BILLY *starts to get up to go for* TRINA. *She exits.*)

BILLY. (*Leans back. To* ANN.) Trina's such a little bitch, I can't believe she's not my own daughter.

ANN. (*Crossing Down to sofa Left.*) Well, Billy, you *were* pretty dazzling last night. Boy, were you dazzling. Hup!

(*Snaps fingers. He raises his legs as she sits. She pushes them down, places her legs across his comfortably. This action is performed as smoothly as an old dance routine.*)

BILLY. My God, what a scene! Dancing the night away. *Me* with Granny Maud.

ANN. (*Starts to eat an apple.*) Nobody forced you.

BILLY. *Eddy* forced me. I didn't want to go on the town. Eddy *forced* me. He insisted he wanted me. (*Imitating* EDDY.) Billy boy, Mrs. Hayes, little lady, sonny . . . We're going on the town. The party's on Big Ed. (*Back to normal.*) He wanted us.

ANN. He *wanted* to be polite. He *wanted* to make a good impression on *me*. That's what he *wanted*. But you and Mother—

BILLY. Why pick on Maud and me? Trina and young Peter certainly stayed the course. (*Pause.*) He's quite an attractive boy, isn't he?

ANN. (*Starts to take a bite of apple, stops.*) No.

BILLY. No? I thought he was quite attractive. Very poised.

ANN. He's not attractive to *me*.

BILLY. I thought he was very attractive. Very poised.

ANN. He's too poised.

BILLY. Is he Trina's new thing?

ANN. What else?

BILLY. Oh, I don't know. (*Joking.*) Maybe as Mama gets older, she fancies 'em younger.

ANN. (*Furious.*) What a filthy little showbiz mind . . . (*Takes one of* BILLY's *moccasins off and starts to go for him with it.*)

BILLY. Hey. Hey. (*He takes the shoe from her gently but firmly, puts it on her foot over her own shoe.*) Hey, wait a minute! I'm *sorry*.

ANN. You can be the most tasteless . . .

BILLY. Sorry . . .

ANN. There's nothing in the world more revolting than a creaky old lady running after a boy.

BILLY. (*Kindly.*) Come on. You're only thirty-eight.

ANN. (*Mumbles.*) Forty.

BILLY. What?

ANN. Forty!

BILLY. (*Starts to rise with interest.*) Forty? You mean you're older than me?

ANN. (*Leans in.*) You're forty-one.

BILLY. (*Leans in.*) *Thirty-eight!* It's in Celebrity Register. Thirty-eight. Three-eight. (*Traces numbers in the air with his finger.*) Forty-two. (*Leans back.*)

ANN. Forty two?

BILLY. Forget it! (ANN *leans back*.) Anyway, I like that Eddy. He suits me fine. I like him.

ANN. I'm glad. If I ever run into him again I'll tell him.

BILLY. (*Rises to sitting position, puts on shoe.* ANN *sits up.*) Don't kid a kidder, baby. You're seeing him to-night. I *heard*.

ANN. (*Laughs.*) What's it to you?

BILLY. It's time you found somebody to take care of you. Somebody substantial, like Eddy. I wouldn't want you screwing around with some little penny-ante adventurer.

ANN. (*Sincerely.*) Billy, I want you to know how much I truly appreciate your not minding your own business.

BILLY. Stick with me, kid. *And* if the chance presents itself, you might slip in a kind word for little Billy. (*Rises, takes off apron, puts it on coffee table.*)

ANN. (*Still kidding.*) I'll try to find one.

BILLY. (*Suddenly serious.*) I'm not kidding. I need it. (*Crosses to chair Right.*)

ANN. (*Astonished.*) You're not having trouble getting work, are you?

BILLY. (*Starts to put on jacket.*) Not at all, I'm not pushing Richard Burton off the screen, but I think I'll probably survive him.

ANN. Then *what?*

BILLY. Annie, the most extraordinary . . . the most unaccountable . . . *sensations* have been zapping me for the last year . . .

ANN. (*Deeply concerned.*) What *is* it?

BILLY. It comes over me at the damndest times . . . on the set, the cameras grinding away, my nose down some stupid bird's bozoom . . . Suddenly I hear this voice . . . "Is this any way for a grown man to make a living?" (*Crosses Upstage sofa to Down Left.*) Or I'm horsing around with the gang in Vegas. Everybody's having a million laughs. And suddenly I find myself wondering if I wouldn't rather be home with a book . . . I mean a home with an upstairs and a wife and a kid with

remedial reading. I tell you, at first I thought I was losing my effing mind! Annie, I've been putting on makeup
and wearing elevator shoes for over twenty years. Now,
suddenly, for *no reason*, it embarrasses me. I want to
give up acting and go straight.

ANN. *You?* Give up acting? You're too good!

BILLY. (*After a moment's consideration.*) True. But—

ANN. (*Bewildered.*) What on earth could you do?

BILLY. (*Crosses to* ANN *on sofa.*) Well, I thought
maybe Eddy . . . Annie, I want to try to get a job. I
mean, a real job.

ANN. Like what?

BILLY. Public relations?

ANN. (*Dubiously.*) Public relations? Is that real?

BILLY. (*Crossly.*) I've got to start somewhere. What
do you want me to do, go cold turkey? (*Starts for the
bar.*) I think I'll have a drink.

ANN. (*Shakes her head.*) No. You're going home.

BILLY. (*Stops.*) Why?

ANN. (*Rises, starts for bedroom.*) Because I'm tireder
than I thought. I want a little rest before Eddy gets here.

BILLY. Ah. I accept that. Make yourself gorgeous. You
know, that couple of pounds you put on during your vaca-
tion are very nicely distributed. Eddy looks like a guy
who would go for the curves.

ANN. Billy, a forty-year-old woman doesn't need a
stage mother.

BILLY. Forty years old! Don't think like that—think
like a diamond.

ANN. What?

BILLY. Not years—carats. You are a multi-carated,
blue-white—

(*PHONE rings.*)

ANN. Ah! That must be Harry Winston. (*PHONE
rings again. She answers it. Into phone.*) Hello? . . .
Oh, Eddy! . . . (BILLY *crosses to desk chair, sits. She*

immediately takes his arm, pushes him to sofa. He sits on Right arm of sofa.) Oh, I did too. The party was just marvelous. And wildly extravagant. What time tonight? (*Listens for a moment, her face falling.*) Oh, I see. Well, if you can't make it, you can't.

BILLY. (*Rises, goes to her, speaks sotto voce.*) What's he trying to pull?

ANN. (*Covers mouthpiece.*) Don't be such a pimp! (*Into phone.*) What about tomorrow? . . . Oh? For the whole week? (BILLY *sits again.*) Well, have a good trip. . . . Please don't apologize! I'll talk to you when you get back . . . Goodbye. (*She hangs up.*)

BILLY. The balloon go up?

ANN. He's been called to the coast on business. You surely don't want him to neglect *your future!* (*Shrugs.*) I'll fix you something to eat.

BILLY. (*Looks at watch.*) Well, actually, Ann—

ANN. Are *you* going to walk out on me too?

BILLY. (*Sincerely.*) I've got a goddam date. (*Rises.*)

ANN. (*Crosses Down Right.*) I should know better than to count on you for anything.

BILLY. Honey, I've had this date all week!

ANN. So who's the lucky girl?

BILLY. Elke.

ANN. Elke . . .

BILLY. You remember Elke.

ANN. Elke? Who works upstairs? That big blonde knockwurst?

BILLY. (*Cutting in.*) That *gorgeous* big blonde knockwurst.

ANN. (*Going to him.*) Billy, it's very disrespectful for you to sleep with the help in my *building.* This is a *co-op.* (*Sits in chair Right.*) And since you're now so adult, you really ought to give up mothers' helpers. I see her in the elevator all the time. She lets the kid's nose run! She looks feeble-minded. She's a minor. How old is she, anyway?

BILLY. Almost nineteen.

ANN. That's rotten!

BILLY. What is?

ANN. You are seducing an under-aged, feeble-minded, kindersitter! *Why?*

BILLY. (*Thoughtfully.*) She don't fight back.

ANN. You old goat. (*She throws a pillow at him.*)

BILLY. (*Tosses pillow on sofa.*) Part of the growing-up process I was describing to you is this marvelous goatish thing for helpless young girls. I guess it's maturity. (*Crosses to door.*)

ANN. (*Breaks down, laughs.*) Oh, Billy, beat it. Everything's so utterly ridiculous.

BILLY. (*He opens door, goes, then pokes his head back in.*) I really am sorry about tonight. (*He goes.*)

ANN. Okay. Okay. Okay. (*She rises.*) Okay . . . (*She replaces pillow on chair, goes to bar, picks up bottle of ouzo, puts it back, starts to hum Greek theme melody, does a little dance step toward the sofa, picks up apple, starts to eat it as she lies down, turns on the TELE-VISION set listlessly, reaches over, turns on lamp Up-stage of sofa. We hear less than half a minute of the Pan-Am jingle: "Pan-Am makes the going great," etc., then the* ANNOUNCER'S VOICE.)

ANNOUNCER'S VOICE. Yes, Pan-Am makes the going great. Go with Pan-Am and you'll go where the action is. This is the blue Aegean with its lovely, romantic islands. Let a Pan-Am ticket take you there. Go where the action is. Go where it's happening. Go, go, go.

ANN. (*Snapping off the SET.*) I went! (*She sighs. The DOORBELL rings. She goes to the door, opens it. It is* PETER. ANN *starts to shut the door. He pushes it back open.*) You can't *force* your way in here . . .

PETER. For Chrissake, Ann, this is so bloody *undigni-fied* . . .

ANN. Please. I'm not alone. (*She turns, backs up against the door.*) Mother's in her room.

PETER. No she's not. (*Pushes his way in.*) I saw her go out just past noon. *And* Trina. (*Crosses Down Left.*) I've been waiting hours for that bastard Boylan to leave. Where is he?

ANN. He's got a girl friend in the building.

PETER. (*Looks at her questioningly.*) Do you care?

ANN. I just didn't expect to have to spend the evening alone.

PETER. Well, now you don't.

ANN. (*She looks at him thoughtfully, closes door, makes up her mind to attempt reason.*) Peter . . . Sit down, Peter. I want to talk to you.

PETER. Okay. I want to talk to you too. (*Sits Right end of sofa.*)

ANN. (*Crosses Down Right.*) Now, Peter. This has got to stop. You know that. You are a very intelligent boy. You're even a rather sensitive boy. (*Starts Left Upstage of sofa.*) You have a way of . . . a kind of natural authority that is . . . (*Reaching for a word.*)

PETER. (*Helping.*) Very unusual.

ANN. (*Left of sofa.*) Very unusual in a . . .

PETER. (*Continuing to feed her.*) In a lad of my years.

ANN. (*Picking it up.*) In a lad of your . . . *Don't mock me.* (*He puts left leg comfortably up on sofa.*) Now, Peter. Since you are intelligent *and* sensitive . . . you must have some *small* . . . some small . . . (*Again reaching for a word.*)

PETER AND ANN. (*Together.*) Insight.

ANN. Yes. Some small insight into my position . . . (*She sits on sofa Left, starts to put her legs over his, as she had done previously with Billy. She is horrified as she realizes her error, immediately puts her feet back on the floor.*) my *feelings.* It must be obvious . . . at least I *hope* it is . . . that I am a respectable woman . . . (PETER *reaches for her hand. She moves Left on the sofa. He follows.*) I mean I know what happened . . . what happened in Greece . . . *Nevertheless* . . .

(PETER *leans over and kisses her firmly but gently to*

stem the flow of words. When he moves back, she just sits quietly.)

PETER. May I speak now? (*She whimpers.*) Ann . . . (*He rises, crosses Down Right, turns back.*) by the time I was ten I'd had four passports. My mother buzzed around a lot and I'll say this for her, she was always ready to yank me along with her. I wasn't left to the servants. My old man's kind of a standard son of a bitch and my mother—

ANN. Oh, Peter. I'm sure I remind you of your mother. You may not have been conscious of it, but—

PETER. I've never known a woman who reminded me less of my mother.

ANN. Huh?

PETER. You know who reminds me of my mother? *Trina* reminds me of my mother.

ANN. (*Laughs, then turns serious.*) Oh, God.

PETER. All I'm trying to say is that I'm only twenty-two . . .

ANN. (*Softly.*) I know.

PETER. . . . but I've been around. I've had my quota of girls . . . and their mothers . . .

ANN. Do you spare the grannies?

PETER. (*Sees her shocked expression, crosses Right two steps.*) You're an astonishingly unsophisticated woman, you know. (*Grins.*) Very middle-class—

ANN. (*A small smile.*) You are ridiculous.

PETER. You're smiling. That's the first time you've really smiled at me. Do you like for me to be ridiculous? It's easy.

ANN. Peter . . . I don't know what to say. I'm very touched and absolutely *horrified.*

PETER. Why?

ANN. Because I had no idea. Peter, I *cannot* let you come here again.

PETER. I think you're right about that. We'll take an apartment . . .

(*She rises, crosses Left two steps.* PETER *follows.*)

ANN. Peter . . . I want you to go now.

PETER. No, that's not what you want.

ANN. I mean it!

PETER. In all the hoo-ha around here, I think I forgot to tell you that I am in love with you.

ANN. (*Speechless for a moment.*) I'm very honored. And terribly flattered. (*He tries to take her hands, she evades him. Starts Right Upstage of sofa; he follows her slowly.*) But Peter, for you to be in love with me, it just isn't . . . *convenient.* You can't just . . . *fling* yourself into my life like some crazy . . . sit-in! (*Right of sofa.*) Every time I move I have to step over *you.* You're up-setting things. My life has a certain . . . a certain balance . . . and harmony—

PETER. You'd be better off with a little chaos.

ANN. Well, you certainly provide that!

PETER. It's the youth bit. (*Smiles engagingly. Crosses to her near chair Right.*) Spontaneity, say what you mean, mean what you feel . . . "Pow!" . . . Action now. You'll learn to love it.

ANN. No. No, I won't. Don't you understand I've *had* all that . . . that "Pow! Action now" business. What I want is— (*Softly.*) "Pow!" . . . *tranquility* now. (*She sits on Right arm of chair.*)

PETER. How about trying for "dead"?

ANN. I *mean* it.

PETER. I don't believe you.

ANN. Then believe *this.* I am not attracted to young boys. Not you, not *any.*

PETER. Lady, that is a lie. I don't know about anybody else, but you are certainly attracted to *me.* Why can't you be honest? What are you so frightened of?

ANN. It's horrible!

PETER. What is?

ANN. (*Rises, turns out.*) Falling all over a young man—

PETER. But you're not falling all over me.

ANN. *Not yet!* (*Turns to him, realizes what she has revealed, turns out front again.*)

PETER. Well, that was honest.

ANN. (*Turns back to him.*) *I am not in love with you.*

PETER. You don't know whether you are or not. You haven't given yourself a chance. You're so spooked by the idea of what "People Will Think," you can't think yourself. Listen, Ann . . . (*He crosses to Center.*) who are all those people whose opinions count so much? Your mother? Your daughter? Mayor Lindsay? Your mother's charming but she wouldn't care if I were still in short pants as long as she hooks up with the Hohenhausers!

ANN. Why, you arrogant—

PETER. (*Going on.*) As for Trina—

ANN. Please go.

PETER. You are a beautiful and desirable woman . . . (*Crosses to her.*) I love you, Ann . . . Let me love you. (*He takes her in his arms. They embrace.*)

ANN. (*Pulling away as she hears KEY in the front door.*) Oh, God! It's my mother!

(*She yanks away from him, assuming a carefree attitude, totally spurious.* PETER *straightens his tie.* MAUD *enters in coat and hat.*)

MAUD. (*Sees* PETER.) Why, good evening, Peter. (*Crosses Down Right.*)

PETER. Good evening, Mrs. Hayes. I just dropped in—

ANN. Unfortunately, Trina isn't in.

MAUD. But you'll wait for her, won't you?

ANN. You mustn't try to keep him, Mother. He's already said he had to leave—

MAUD. Oh, what a pity. Trina will be utterly shattered at having missed you!

ANN. Yes.

PETER. (*Shakes her hand.*) Good night, Mrs. Hayes. I'm glad I at least got a glimpse of *you* . . . (*To* ANN.) Good night. (*Crosses to door.*)

ANN. (*Follows him.*) Good night, Peter.

MAUD. (*Sits on Right arm of sofa, starts to take off hat, gloves, unbuttons coat.*) Come back soon. You're part of the family now. We've adopted you!

ANN. (*Opening the door.*) Good night.

(PETER *kisses her hand.* MAUD *is not watching; she's busy with her gloves, hat, etc.* PETER *keeps kissing both of* ANN'S *hands. She tries to push him out the door, but he playfully keeps kissing her hands. She finally gets him out the door. His hands still show and she's trying to avoid closing the door on his hands. She keeps pushing his hands the way one does with a cat's paws when trying to put the cat in a traveling box. She finally succeeds in getting his hands outside and closes the door. She stands facing the door for a moment.*)

MAUD. Has he been here long?

ANN. Huh?

MAUD. Has he been here long?

ANN. Who?

MAUD. Peter.

ANN. (*Crosses Down Right.*) A few minutes.

MAUD. Of course he's courting you like mad!

ANN. (*Stops, looks at her Mother.*) Why would he be courting me?

MAUD. Because he's after Trina.

ANN. Oh.

MAUD. I think he's quite smitten with her.

ANN. You do?

MAUD. Why can't that silly Trina stay home occasionally? (*Rises.*) Oh, I'm so glad I'm not that age, anymore. Aren't you? (*She goes.*)

ANN. (*Looks in mirror, crosses down, sits on sofa, picks up apple from coffee table. Then in a small, wistful voice, sings softly.*) M-I-C, K-E-Y, M-O-U-S-EEE . . .

(FIVE-COUNT LIGHT FADE ON "MOUSE")

BLACKOUT

(ROCK 'N' ROLL MUSIC)

ACT ONE

SCENE 7

ANN's *apartment. A month later. Evening.*

TRINA *is on the sofa, doing her homework. She is wearing large sunglasses. The radio is playing rock 'n' roll MUSIC very loud.* MAUD *enters from hall carrying a large basket of flowers, crosses Upstage sofa, turns off RADIO.*

TRINA. Please don't turn that off. I'm doing my homework.

MAUD. (*Puts flowers on card table.*) Trina, I want to talk to you about Peter.

TRINA. Again?

MAUD. (*Crosses Upstage sofa to Right, sits.*) I want to know if you think he's in love with you.

TRINA. (*Shrugs.*) How should I know?

MAUD. If you don't, I can't think who does! Don't you at least have an opinion?

TRINA. In my opinion, Peter is not in love with me.

MAUD. How does he behave when you're alone?

TRINA. We're never alone . . . If you're not here, Mummy is . . . Or if we go out—which isn't very often —it's always with Arthur or some other kids.

MAUD. You went dancing night before last . . . At least you dance alone—you know, cheek-to-cheek.

TRINA. What-to-what?

MAUD. Don't be coarse! Well, at least you talk to each other. What does he talk about?

TRINA. The whole point of the Electric Circus is you don't have to talk. You can't. It's bombs bursting in air!

MAUD. Charming.

TRINA. It's super.

MAUD. (*A pause.*) He brings you home. What happens when he brings you home?

TRINA. Nothing.

MAUD. He doesn't kiss you?

TRINA. No.

MAUD. I don't believe it! My word! You don't suppose he's . . . "you-know"?

TRINA. No, he's not.

MAUD. How can you tell?

TRINA. I asked him.

MAUD. (*Horrified.*) You asked him! Why, you little idiot!

TRINA. (*Gathers books from floor, rises.*) Granny Maud, I think you ought to just settle down and accept the fact that Peter is not in love with me. You're never going to be related to the Hohenhausers. He doesn't dig me . . . I don't appeal to him. (*Upstage Left of sofa.*)

MAUD. But you're the living image of me!

TRINA. Then *you* don't appeal to him.

MAUD. Nonsense. He adores me. He's just shy. He needs encouragement.

TRINA. (*She crosses Right of* MAUD, *near desk. Comforts her.*) Granny, I'm only seventeen. The world is full of attractive and eligible men. I'm not going to push the panic button because one of them doesn't drop dead at my feet.

MAUD. Peter Latham can provide you with every luxury you can think of, and a great many you've never heard of.

(*DOORBELL rings.*)

TRINA. Saved by the bell!

MAUD. (*Rising.*) Trina, please go to your room.

TRINA. Why?

MAUD. (*Crosses to door.*) That's Peter. And I want to talk to him. If you won't give the poor boy a little help, *I* will.

TRINA. (*Shrugs, starts for her room.*) If I were you, I wouldn't get mixed up in this. (*She goes.*)

(MAUD *opens the door and* PETER *enters. He hands* MAUD *a pretty box.*)

MAUD. Ah . . .

PETER. Hello, Mrs. Hayes. I brought you some *marrons glacés.*

MAUD. (*Fondly.*) You really do spoil us, Peter. Trina's mother adores *marrons glacés.* (*Crosses Down, puts box on coffee table.*)

PETER. Oh, does she? I just took a chance that somebody would. (*Crosses Down Left to card table.*) She—uh—hasn't come home yet?

MAUD. No. I'm alone. We can play without a soul to bother us. (*Moves flowers from card table to coffee table.*)

PETER. Great. (PETER *indicates basket of flowers.*) Somebody's birthday?

MAUD. (*Sits Right of card table.*) No, no. That darling Eddy Edwards sent them.

PETER. (*Sits across from* MAUD.) Is *he* back again?

MAUD. Just this morning. (*Deals the cards; looks at* PETER *as she does so, approvingly.*) My, what a good-looking suit. Aren't you grand!

PETER. The old man was in town today. We had lunch.

MAUD. He must be very proud of you. You take your position in the company very seriously. (*Finishes dealing.*) Basically, I feel you are a very serious person. (*They begin to play gin rummy.*) Wouldn't you say you are?

PETER. About average, I guess.

MAUD. No, much more than average. I'm a very keen judge of character, Peter. Your emotions run *very* deep. (*Looks at him with big eyes.*) Poor Peter . . . (*Sur-*

prised, he looks up from the cards, meets her gaze.) I'm not a complete idiot, you know. I've seen through you for quite a while now. (*It's* PETER'S *turn to draw a card, but he is stunned by what* MAUD *has just said. He draws a card from the deck automatically, and keeps drawing cards, which he puts in his hand without looking and without discarding others.* MAUD *doesn't see any of this and continues speaking.*) I know what's going on, Peter—why you come here so often. And I know it isn't to play gin rummy with an old lady. (*She smiles knowingly.* PETER *keeps drawing. He now has drawn six or seven cards.*) Do you think I'm so old I no longer recognize love when it's right under my nose? (*She now looks at* PETER. *He stops drawing.*)

PETER. (*Cautiously.*) What are you getting at, Mrs. Hayes?

MAUD. Just that I know you're in love and that I'm on your side.

PETER. (*Quite taken aback.*) You are?

MAUD. And I'll do anything I can to help you. You have my promise.

PETER. Mrs. Hayes! I never dreamed you'd see it like that!

MAUD. Of course Trina is terribly young . . .

PETER. Who?

MAUD. Trina. She's terribly young. (PETER *laughs mirthlessly.*) I know, I know. She doesn't seem young. It's a very sophisticated generation. Not like when I was that age . . . or even Ann. Ann was—I can see your cards . . . Ann was awesomely innocent. Sometimes I think she still is.

PETER. Yes.

MAUD. Ann doesn't see things head-on. What will be hard for her to grasp is that age is not the question here. The question is simply what is best for the two individuals involved. You will have to convince her that marriage is possible. Possible and desirable. (PETER *hits the table with his hand.* MAUD *jumps.*) You're knocking?

PETER. No. You were talking about marriage.

MAUD. Of course. If you really love her.

PETER. Oh, I do love her, Mrs. Hayes. But, marriage!
. . . It simply never occurred to me.

MAUD. Peter, I'm shocked!

PETER. Well, there are— uh —obstacles—you know.

MAUD. You're worried about your parents. That they'll
think you're too young.

PETER. (*Slight grimace.*) Well . . .

MAUD. (*Leans towards* PETER.) Can't you bring them
around?

PETER. (*Leans towards* MAUD, *grins.*) It would be interesting to try. But I'm not dependent on my parents.

MAUD. But it would be so much nicer if they did
approve.

PETER. So much nicer.

MAUD. Still, every couple must eventually live for them-
selves. Take a card.

PETER. You believe that?

MAUD. Yes. And you must be very firm with *Ann!* She
may fight you.

PETER. Don't worry, I'll handle Ann.

MAUD. And, Peter dear, let me give you just one more
bit of advice—

(ANN *enters.*)

ANN. I'm home.

MAUD. Gin! (*Slaps her cards face down.* PETER *stares
at* MAUD'S *cards on the table, starts to say something.*
MAUD *cuts him off. She rises, messes up all the cards on
the table.*) It's gin. In spades, and that counts double. If
you'll excuse me, I have to go and make up the menus.
(*Starts Right.*) We can settle up later, Peter. I know I
can trust you. (*Sees* ANN *standing near bar. Pretends
surprise.*) Oh, hello, Ann. (*She goes into hallway.*)

ANN. (*Crossing Down Right.*) What's she up to?
(PETER *is staring at the cards in his hand.*) That's a very
funny look. What's it supposed to mean?

PETER. (*Looking at cards strangely.*) I've got seven-teen cards! (*Puts them down.*)

ANN. (*Crossing to coffee table, picks up flowers, puts them on card table.*) La! What a splendid suit! (*Teasing.*) Playing grown-up?

PETER. (*Unflappable.*) About the same as everybody else. When did the Big Wind from the West blow back in?

ANN. (*Crossing down to sofa.*) Ah! That's what's eating you.

PETER. I just asked you if you'd seen the Big Wind.

(ANN *picks up box of* marrons glacés, *turns to him, smiles. He nods; she puts them down, sits at Left end of sofa.*)

ANN. Would you mind fixing me a drink?

PETER. (*Goes Upstage sofa to bar, looks towards hall-way to be sure* MAUD *is out of earshot.*) You're pretty late.

ANN. (*Tiredly.*) Oh, there were a million rotten things at the office.

PETER. (*At bar, mixing drink.*) Why do you do it?

ANN. (*Annoyed.*) Why do I . . . I've got bad habits. I like to eat.

PETER. (*A beat.*) You could get married.

ANN. I've been married.

PETER. Not to me.

ANN. (*Looks at him briefly, decides to make a joke of it.*) I can't marry you, Peter. It's against the teachings of my church.

PETER. (*Crosses to her.*) The teachings of what church?

ANN. The Over-Thirty Orthodox.

PETER. (*Hands her drink.*) I'm not kidding, Ann. I'm asking you. Will you marry me?

ANN. I'm not kidding, Peter. I'm telling you. No.

PETER. (*Quietly.*) Why?

ANN. Because I know what would happen.

PETER. What would happen?

ANN. You know how old I am.

PETER. (*Turns away Right, impatiently.*) Oh, God! Look. Suppose you were thirty-five. Would you marry me if you were thirty-five? (*Moves in behind her.*)

ANN. No.

PETER. Thirty?

ANN. No.

PETER. Twenty-nine?

ANN. (*Starts to say no, stops.*) I don't think so . . . no, of course I wouldn't.

PETER. *Twenty-five?*

ANN. (*Hesitates, then smiles.*) I'd be tempted.

PETER. You know you would.

ANN. I might.

PETER. So let's suppose you're twenty-five and we get married. Then what happens?

ANN. (*Sharply.*) How do *I* know?

PETER. (*Leans towards her.*) *Exactly.*

ANN. (*Puzzled, then annoyed.*) How does anyone know what will happen in a marriage—or in life?

PETER. *Exactly.* (ANN *slowly begins to understand what he's trying to say.*) All anybody ever really has is *now.*

ANN. (*There is a moment of silence, then she takes a deep breath. Starts for bedroom, turns, heads for kitchen.*) Peter, please go. This is my night to . . . (*Reaching.*) I've really got to polish the silver.

PETER. (*Follows her Left.*) All right. But while you're polishing the silver, will you think about it? And try to think about yourself. Nobody else.

ANN. (*Still bewildered.*) I'll try.

PETER. (*He kisses her, goes up to door and turns back.*) Okay, go on, polish the silver. (*He goes.*)

(ANN *stands there lost in thought for a moment.* MAUD, *followed by* TRINA, *enters from hallway, crosses to Upstage sofa.*)

MAUD. Did I hear Peter leave? What did he say?

TRINA. What did Peter say to you?

ANN. (*Puzzled.*) About what?

TRINA. I guess you know that Granny practically put a shotgun in his back!

ANN. (*Stares at* MAUD.) Mother! What on earth did you say to him?

MAUD. (*Very pleased with herself.*) I simply brought it to his attention that his feelings were perfectly obvious to me and that I thoroughly approved. And I said I wanted to know his intentions.

ANN. Oh, you did.

MAUD. He was surprised.

ANN. He was surprised.

MAUD. But when I said I thought he should speak to you, he very quickly agreed. (*Silence.*) Well? What happened? Did he declare himself?

ANN. He *certainly did.*

TRINA. (*Starts Left.*) Look, Mummy—

MAUD. (*Stopping her, impatiently.*) Please be quiet, Trina. I'm trying to talk to your mother about Peter.

TRINA. It's not *you* he wants to marry, Granny. It's *me.*

ANN. (*Gazes from* MAUD *to* TRINA.) Actually . . . actually, (*Crosses to end of sofa.*) what he's got in mind is something in between—a kind of compromise. (*Sits on sofa.*) Well, let's put it this way . . .

FAST CURTAIN

ACT TWO

SCENE 1

ANN's *apartment, a few days later. It is evening.*

ANN *and* EDDY *are alone.* ANN, *wearing a kaftan-style housecoat, is Upstage sofa, demonstrating different colors and swatches of fabric.* EDDY *is standing Down Right.*

ANN. (*Dramatically throwing first one then another large sample of fabric across the back of the sofa.*) Which do you like? The plum? or the aubergine?

EDDY. (*Looking confused.*) Uh . . . Which is the plum and which is the aubergine?

ANN. *This* is the aubergine. *I* like the plum.

EDDY. (*Sycophantically.*) *I* like the plum. It's perfect! I don't see how you do it! I can't even pick out the right tie. (ANN *gives a little grin.*) Oh, I guess you noticed. I always depended on my wife for things like that . . . (*Sighs.*) I'm mighty grateful for your advice, Ann. This apartment's sure gonna have your brand on it.

ANN. (*Laughs, sits on sofa Left.*) Oh, Eddy.

EDDY. (*Crossing Down Left.*) You've been so nice about the little apartment . . . I wonder how you'd feel about taking on something a shade bigger . . .

ANN. What did you have in mind, Eddy?

EDDY. (*Crosses Upstage sofa to Down Right chair.*) Something out in the country. Maybe Connecticut. Something you could . . . kind of . . . *expand* in. (*Shyly.*) Something maybe a woman might like. Something, say, *you'd* like. I mean to your *taste.*

(*He turns to her.* ANN *is suddenly very uncomfortable.*)

56

ANN. I've changed my mind about the plum.

EDDY. I sure wish you'd hear me out, Ann.

ANN. Although the aubergine—

EDDY. I was pretty lost after my wife died.

ANN. Yes, yes, I'm sure you were. But Eddy—

EDDY. I don't want you to misunderstand me. I'm not trying to pass myself off as something special . . . Matter of fact, I guess if my wife hadn't been sick—all those years—I would have cut out.

ANN. It must have been very hard on you.

EDDY. (*Sits Right end of sofa, shrugs.*) Oh, well. You just do what you have to. But that's all finished and done. Ann . . .

(*Takes her hand. The kitchen door opens and* MAUD *appears, crosses Downstage of the coffee table.*)

MAUD. Ann, do we want that casserole—? (*Sees* ANN *and* EDDY.) Oh, Eddy, I didn't know you were still here . . . (*Crosses to Right, then up toward hallway.*) Oh, please, don't let me disturb you. Continue! Continue!

(EDDY *rises politely.* MAUD *exits Up Right.*)

EDDY. (*Sits again.*) Yeah. Well, like I was saying . . . It may sound funny coming from a man who admits he wasn't much of a husband the first time out . . . but I swear to you, I could make a woman happy. The *right* woman.

ANN. (*Trying to get in.*) Oh, I'm convi—

EDDY. I'd give her everything. She'd be a regular little queen. What I want above everything else is a family. My wife—my late wife—couldn't have children. I don't think a man's lived his life unless he leaves children. I'd like to have . . . Hell! I'll take as many as I can get! (*Laughs.*)

ANN. (*She also laughs, but nervously.*) I see.

EDDY. I'm only forty-five and at forty-five, a man is at

his peak! And I just *know* I'll make a good husband for Trina.

ANN. Trina?

EDDY. Trina will make some little mother! That kid of yours.

ANN. Some little mother. Have you alerted Trina to this *project?*

EDDY. We love each other, Ann.

ANN. (*Rises, crosses Left three steps.*) I see.

EDDY. We want to get married right away. We don't see any point in waiting around.

ANN. (*Politely.*) Certainly not with you at your peak. How long has this been going on?

EDDY. (*Rises, crosses Right.*) Well, to tell you the truth . . . you may not like this but . . . ever since that first night—the night we all went out together. It happened just like that.

ANN. But you kept it secret? That wasn't very nice, Eddy.

EDDY. I know that. It's been about to drive me crazy. But Trina was so sure you . . . that you'd . . .

ANN. That I'd what?

EDDY. I've never been around girls Trina's age— I mean around them and their mothers . . . I didn't know what to believe. Trina was so sure you'd be . . . (*Forces himself.*) *Jealous.* Hell! Trina thinks just because *she's* interested in me, every other woman is too. (*Chuckles.*) She's such a kid.

ANN. Yes, she is. Too much of a kid for marriage.

EDDY. Why? The way I see it, a woman of eighteen—

ANN. Trina's only seventeen.

EDDY. (*Surprised.*) She *is?* (*Rather pleased.*) Why the little devil. (*Laughs.*) Well, the way I see it, a woman of . . . seventeen, eighteen . . . and a man of forty-five are a perfect balance.

ANN. Maybe in the Ozarks, Eddy. But not in this zip code.

EDDY. I love her, Ann.

ANN. (*Crosses Left.*) Oh, for God's sake! If you're fool enough to let yourself fall in love with a seventeen— (*Stops herself.*)

EDDY. If I'm a fool, well, I'll just have to live with it.

ANN. Fine. And Trina will live with me.

EDDY. (*Crosses Left to her.*) You're going to find Trina's made up her own mind about where she's going to live.

ANN. Eddy . . . how would you like ten to twenty in the state pen?

EDDY. (*Takes her shoulders.*) You've got a lot to think about, Ann. I'm going to run along. (*Starts for door.*)

ANN. Now wait a minute, Eddy.

EDDY. (*Blandly going on. At door.*) And, honey, you just bear in mind what good care I'll take of Trina. And of you too.

ANN. Of me?

EDDY. Naturally. I'm going to be your son-in-law. (EDDY *goes.*)

ANN. (*Crosses Upstage sofa to near bar. Calls out.*) *Trina!*

(TRINA *appears immediately, goes to* ANN.)

TRINA. I might as well tell you right now, Mummy, that if you pull something square like trying to keep me from seeing Eddy, I'll just talk him into taking me to Tahiti or some place out of your reach until I'm eighteen and then we'll be married anyway.

ANN. (*Cutting in.*) You are playing Juliet to a fairly sedate Romeo.

TRINA. (*Coolly.*) I shouldn't think you'd want me to answer that in kind, Mummy.

ANN. (*Trying to stay calm. Crosses Down Left to sofa.*) Trina, my big mistake was not sending you to a good, tough military school.

TRINA. (*Crossing Downstage.*) I'm going to marry Eddy.

ANN. Do you love him?

TRINA. I think so.

ANN. You think so.

TRINA. He's crazy about me. He makes all the decisions. It's so easy to be with him. You thought Eddy was nice enough for *you,* didn't you?

ANN. I wasn't contemplating marrying Eddy.

TRINA. (*Crosses to below coffee table.*) You don't contemplate marrying *anybody.* You'd have let Eddy hang around just the way you let a kid like Peter. Just hang around. Only Eddy would never have asked you to marry him because you'd have brushed him off long before he got to the point. Because *he's* too *possible.* He's a darling man, and I decided I'd be damned if I'd let you waste *him.* So I swiped him. (*Sits in chair Right.*)

ANN. (*Crosses Right three steps.*) So you swiped him.

TRINA. Right from under your nose, Mummy.

ANN. (*Crosses to* TRINA.) That couldn't have been so hard, Trina. I mean you are very young and very lovely. Any mother who thinks of competing with her daughter has lost before she starts.

TRINA. Oh, I don't know. There's Peter.

ANN. Did you want Peter?

TRINA. It wouldn't have mattered much if I had.

ANN. If you had, then what?

TRINA. Tough beans, that's what. (ANN *crosses Upstage sofa.*) Anyway, (*Rises.*) I don't want Peter, I want Eddy.

ANN. Why? Why Eddy?

TRINA. I told you! He's great. He takes care of me.

ANN. Trina, I've taken care of you.

TRINA. I'm sorry, Mummy, but you just don't make it as a father image.

ANN. (*Crosses Down Left of sofa.*) Oh, boy!

TRINA. (*Goes to* ANN.) Oh, forget it, Mummy. You've done okay.

ANN. Oh, Trina, have I?

(*They embrace.*)

TRINA. Well, you let me run all over you, of course, but you're so sweet that whenever you *try* to stand up to me, I make it a point to give in. If it's not too important.

(MAUD *risks a glance through the hallway.*)

MAUD. Is he gone? (*Not seeing* EDDY, *comes into room, crosses Up Right sofa.* TRINA *crosses Right three steps.*) Well! What was *that* all about? I obviously walked in in the middle of *something.*

ANN. What you walked in in the middle of was a proposal.

MAUD. *Eddy?* Oh, Ann! (*Crosses to* ANN, *embraces her warmly.*) Oh, my precious girl! I'm so happy for you!

ANN. (*Gently disentangling herself.*) Mother . . . It's not me Eddy wants to marry, Mother—it's Trina.

MAUD. (*Disengages herself after a moment.*) What? What in the world is *wrong* with everybody? Everyone's gone mad! Or is it *me?* (*Doing a complete about-face, crosses to* TRINA.) Trina! My darling girl! I'm so happy for you! (*It is* TRINA *who now suffers* MAUD's *embrace.*)

BLACKOUT

(*ROCK 'N' ROLL MUSIC*)

ACT TWO

SCENE 2

ANN's *office, a few days later, around noon.*

MRS. MARGOLIN *and* BILLY *are on Stage. She is sitting at desk, typing. He is sitting in chair in front of desk. Her coat and bag are on rack.*

BILLY. *Trina* and *Eddy.*

MRS. MARGOLIN. They've set the date.

BILLY. Little Trina and Big Ed. I can't believe it! (*Cheerfully.*) At least he's still in the family. I think I'll enjoy having a rich son-in-law.

MRS. MARGOLIN. Mr. Boylan!

BILLY. I take a European view of these things, Margy. "*Honi soit qui mal y pense.*"

MRS. MARGOLIN. Huh?

BILLY. Never give a sucker an even break.

(ANN *enters from her office. She is carrying a file which she places on* MRS. MARGOLIN'S *desk.*)

ANN. Here are the plans for the Gordonson place. (*Crosses to* BILLY.) Hi, Billy. Glad you could make it. (*Puts her hands on his shoulders.*)

BILLY. I've just heard the news from— (*Pointing to* MRS. MARGOLIN.) Walter Cronkite here. Is that what you wanted to see me about?

ANN. I just wanted to talk to you a bit.

MRS. MARGOLIN. (*Being tactful.*) I think I'll have an early lunch. (*Rises, gets coat and bag, starts for the door.*) I'll be about an hour and a half, if you don't mind. (*Looks at them.*)

ANN. It's all right.

MRS. MARGOLIN. (*At door.*) I thought maybe I'd look for something to give the little bride. I may stop in at F.A.O. Schwarz. (*She goes.*)

BILLY. How's the morale, little buddy? Not zonked?

ANN. I'm not at all zonked!

BILLY. That's the spirit.

ANN. (*Crosses Left.*) Oh, Billy . . . don't treat me as if I'd been left waiting at the altar. The big Eddy romance was all in *your* mind . . . and Mrs. Margolin's . . . and Maud's. *I* was never interested in Eddy! I was just helping him out.

BILLY. Well, he's got Trina to help him now.

ANN. But who's going to help Trina?

BILLY. Haven't you noticed yet that Trina helps herself? Look . . . This is the best thing that could have happened to Trina. *And* you. I think Trina was right on the edge of giving you a hard time. You have lucked out.

ANN. Billy! He's *twenty-eight* years older than she is! It's grotesque!

BILLY. Why?

ANN. (*Crosses Upstage desk to Left.*) You don't think it is?

BILLY. No. He's a very lively fellow . . . Trina's quite mature in many ways . . . It's a perfectly natural attraction. (*Rises, crosses Left three steps.*) Actually, Ann, you'd be surprised how devastating younger girls find *me* . . . There's something very sexy about this age . . .

ANN. (*Almost to herself.*) Have you noticed that, too?

BILLY. (*Stops.*) Too?

ANN. (*Crosses to desk, sits.*) What if I told you that *I've* had a proposal?

BILLY. (*Steps to desk.*) *You? No!* Who?

ANN. Me! Yes! Peter Latham *who!*

BILLY. Peʻer Latham! You mean that *kid? Trina's* little boy friend?

ANN. He's not Trina's little boy friend. He's *my* little boy friend.

BILLY. And he's asked *you* to marry him? (*Crosses up to file, howls with laughter. Goes back to desk.*) What's he on? You've got to keep your eyes open with kids that age.

ANN. I'm so grateful for your solicitude, Billy dear. But I've known Peter for quite some time. He is not on drugs. He is extremely intelligent, holds down a responsible position in the family business . . . Hohenhauser *Steel*, that is.

BILLY. Well, sure. But—

ANN. (*Going on.*) He has money of his own, a mind of his own and he wants to marry *me*. Raddled, old broken-down, liver-spotty *me!* He's even met you and Maud and he *still* wants to marry me.

BILLY. (*He stares open-mouthed for a long moment, then he crosses Left a few steps. Crosses back to desk.*) He must have a thing about his mother. Has he talked much about his mother?

ANN. He says she's very like Trina.

BILLY. (*Crosses Down Left of desk.*) Annie! You don't mean you're taking this seriously! He's a baby! A little, bitty baby! (*Holding his hand about a foot from the floor.*)

ANN. He's twenty-two. Were you a baby at twenty-two?

BILLY. You're damn right I was. A little, bitty baby! (*Repeating hand gesture and kicking the imaginary baby.*)

ANN. Well, he isn't.

BILLY. (*Peers at her.*) Are you *serious?* I can't believe it!

ANN. (*Grimly.*) Believe it.

BILLY. But . . . Jesus, honey! Have you thought—

ANN. What people would say?

BILLY. Yes.

ANN. (*She rises, steps Right, pretends she's entering a cafe with Peter.*) If *you* saw us—and you didn't know us —if you saw Peter and me together in some public place, what would you think?

BILLY. (*Looking at the "couple."*) I'd think you were shelling out.

ANN. Do I look—like the kind of woman who—"shells out"?

BILLY. No, of course you don't, Annie— I didn't mean that.

ANN. I don't think we look too utterly ridiculous together. I check mirrors constantly . . . I mean . . . if we go anywhere. People don't *stare* at us, Billy. (BILLY *turns away Left a few steps. She sits on corner of desk.*) I don't know if you are aware of it, but the latest statistics prove that a woman comes into her full sexual flowering at forty, while a man attains his at twenty.

BILLY. (*Reaching for her.*) So you're in full flower, eh, kid? Give us a whiff—

(ANN *angrily pushes him away.*)

ANN. (*Crosses Right three steps.*) Damn it, I'm serious.

BILLY. (*Stares at her a moment, turns to Center angrily.*) Okay. If the kid is to your taste—what the hell. Youth is great. Enjoy. (*Takes out a cigar.*) We won't talk about it any more.

ANN. (*Goes to him.*) You don't get it. It's not his *youth* that's to my taste. It bothers me terribly. But he's really a marvelous person. He's quite extraordinary. Very strong-*minded.* (*Crosses to desk.*) And he has a good deal of money. Once I stopped to think about it— (*Turns out.*) the overall picture, you understand—it suddenly seemed . . . rather marvelous. I'd given up thinking about . . . well, actually, I guess I kind of put myself out to pasture. And suddenly, here is this handsome, intelligent, *rich, young* man who thinks that *I* . . . am the *greatest.* Billy, he loves me. He could have anybody he wants, and he wants *me.*

BILLY. (*Really, for the first time, believing her. Turns Up Right a few steps, speaks quietly.*) Well—wow.

ANN. (*Crosses to Center.*) Peter wants to *marry* me. Take care of me. It's the damndest thing. But after all these years, after two marriages, I finally find someone strong who— I'm sorry, Billy.

BILLY. That's okay. Say it like it is.

ANN. (*Crosses Left.*) I finally found someone strong who really takes over. And he's a twenty-two-year-old boy.

BILLY. (*Crosses up to file, opens top drawer, leans on it.*) Annushka, you're in *love* with the kid.

ANN. (*Sits on bench.*) Oh, for heaven's sake, Billy. I'm forty years old! It's quite enough to *be* loved. And have a few of my tomorrows taken care of.

BILLY. I see. It's to be a union of love on his part and fatigue on yours. Is that correct?

ANN. I don't want to talk about it any more. Let's go have lunch. (*Rises.*)

BILLY. (*Slams file drawer shut.*) You'll have to forgive me, darling. I seem to have lost my appetite. I'll call you tomorrow.

ANN. All right, tomorrow. (*He starts Left, indicating baby again.*) You're angry.

BILLY. (*Shouts.*) I'm not angry. I'm *never* angry! (*He goes.*)

ANN. (*She reflects a moment, then she moves to the phone with a resolute air, dials.*) Hello . . . Hello, is that you, Peter? . . . Well this is me. And I called to say that, after thinking it over carefully, weighing everything, pro and con, I've decided that . . . Peter, don't interrupt me! . . . Well, *okay!* The answer's *okay!*

BLACKOUT

(*GREEK MUSIC*)

ACT TWO

SCENE 3

Three weeks later. ANN'S *apartment.*

ANN *is offstage in bedroom.* PETER *is standing near bedroom door.*

PETER. But, Ann—

ANN. (*Offstage.*) I can't!

PETER. Ann . . .

ANN. (*Entering from bedroom, crossing up to mirror.*) You can't expect me to! Look at my hair! *I do not want to meet them.*

PETER. Why are you carrying on like this?

ANN. (*Crossing Down Center.*) Because you've given me absolutely no warning. Look at my hair.

PETER. (*Going to her.*) If I'd given you any more warning, you'd have wriggled out of it.

ANN. (*Takes cigarette from coffee table.*) Couldn't it *please* wait until we get back?

PETER. (*Takes cigarette from her, replaces it.*) I want them to meet you before we get married. Look . . . it's better this way—more spontaneous . . . When Mother called this morning and said they were stopping off on their way to Paris, I thought, *now.* Let's get it over with. So I told them.

ANN. (*Crosses Left three steps.*) My God! What a scene that must have—

PETER. I've told you twenty times what their reaction was. They were just . . . (*Lamely.*) surprised. That's all. Surprised.

ANN. Oh, Peter.

PETER. It had to happen sooner or later.

ANN. What's wrong with later? We could have stalled a while. They could have come to my *funeral.* (*Crosses to PETER.*) *Look,* I would have liked a *little* time to prepare myself for . . . this interview.

PETER. It is not an *interview.* You're not applying for a position as an upstairs maid.

ANN. They despise me.

PETER. How can they despise you? They haven't met you. (*He embraces her.*)

ANN. (*A beat, her hand goes to her stomach.*) Peter, I don't feel at all well. (*Crosses to sofa, sits.*) And look at my hair!

PETER. Stop it! You know perfectly well that nothing depends on this visit. We're going to be married next week no matter what. (*Crosses Upstage sofa.*) If this meeting goes down moderately well, everything will be a hell of a lot easier, that's all. And if they don't like it— (*He grins.*) Screw 'em.

ANN. Screw 'em.

PETER. (*Crosses Down Left.*) I'll be interested to see

how you react to the old man. He's something on wheels. Self-made, you know.

ANN. I thought he married— I mean, your mother is a Hohenhauser.

PETER. Oh, that's not the way my father went about it. He grabbed the company away from my grandfather, kicked the old boy into astonished retirement, *then* took over the daughter. Along with everything else in sight.

ANN. My goodness! Your poor grandfather.

PETER. Don't waste your sympathy *there*. My grandfather Hohenhauser was tough and mean and greedy. Bashed his way through a picket line once with a seven-iron. He used to show it to me. Six notches on it. *Still* . . . my father took the old boy on and whipped him and set himself up there as king of the hill before he was thirty-five. (*Grins.*) Wants to know something? He's next.

ANN. You're just a kid.

PETER. (*Steps Right to her.*) Shall I tell you why Dad will be willing to go along with my marrying you? Because he thinks you'll distract *me*. He knows *his* turn is coming up. He feels me breathing down his neck and he's not ready for the axe.

ANN. (*Rather alarmed.*) Oh, Peter, that's—

PETER. Don't worry. I'm giving him five more years. (*Coolly.*) He's five years from retirement. (*The DOOR-BELL rings.* ANN *jumps up, gives a little yelp.* PETER *kisses her briefly, starts for the door.* ANN *crosses Down Left.*) It's okay, lady. You're with me. Fix your hair. (*He opens the door.* MR. *and* MRS. LATHAM *enter.* MR. LATHAM *is very trim with a youthful bearing. She is extremely elegant; she wears the best jewels, the best everything. Very lacquered, in quiet, deadly professional good taste.*) Well, here you are . . . (*Token kiss.*) Mother.

MRS. LATHAM. Darling . . .

PETER. Come in, Dad.

(MRS. LATHAM *crosses Down Right, looking around.* MR. LATHAM *hands* ANN *his hat without looking at her, as though she were the maid. She places the hat on the card table.*)

MRS. LATHAM. Darling, can you believe the coincidence? It's weird. Weird, weird, weird. Aunt Phyllis and I spent two winters in New York right after I came out, and I used to take voice lessons from a Madame Somebody *right here in this very building!* Right here in—

PETER. Mother, I want you to meet Ann. (MRS. LATHAM *turns with a bright smile to* ANN, *crosses to her, hand outstretched.* PETER *crosses Down Left to* ANN.) This is my father, Ann. Mother, this is Ann.

MRS. LATHAM. (*Crossing to* ANN.) Ah, Miss Stanley— Mrs.—?

ANN. Mrs.

MRS. LATHAM. (*Pleasantly.*) *Mrs.* Stanley . . . I'm delighted to meet you.

(*They shake hands.* MR. LATHAM *bows.*)

ANN. I . . . I'm so glad you were able to come.

LATHAM. Peter insisted.

ANN. Yes. Yes, I know he did. (*A moment's silence.*) Please sit down. (LATHAM *sits on sofa.*) Let me fix you a drink.

PETER. (*To* ANN.) Let me do it, Ann. I know what they like. (*Crosses Upstage sofa to bar.*)

MRS. LATHAM. (*Crossing Down Right of sofa.*) What a charming apartment. Sweet . . . and you've decorated it so . . . *bravely.* Sweet, sweet, sweet! (*Gives* LATHAM *a look.*) Edgar?

LATHAM. Sweet.

MRS. LATHAM. (*Picking up a small framed snapshot of* ANN *from the desk.*) What a pretty picture of you. (*Crosses Up Left of sofa.*)

ANN. (*Crossing Right two steps.*) It's . . . quite an old one—

MRS. LATHAM. I used to wear my hair exactly the same

way! (*Sits on back of sofa.*) Remember, Edgar? (*Hands him the picture as she sits.*)

LATHAM. (*He looks at it, then gives it back.*) No.

MRS. LATHAM. Oh, of course you do. I was carrying Peter then . . . (*Crosses to* PETER *at bar.*)

PETER. (*Takes picture from her, puts it on desk again, hands her a drink.*) Mother!

(*She takes the drink, looks momentarily distressed as she realizes she has made a faux pas.*)

LATHAM. Don't fix anything for me, Peter. We haven't enough time.

MRS. LATHAM. (*Crosses, sits on sofa Right.*) Oh, Lord. With Edgar it's always rush, rush, rush.

LATHAM. (*It's obvious that he has decided to speak. Rises, steps to Center, hands in pockets.*) Mrs. Stanley. Actually, I'm glad to have this opportunity to—uh—

(PETER *crosses Down Right.*)

ANN. (*Charmingly.*) Size me up.

LATHAM. (*Laughs.*) Yes. I didn't know what to expect. (*Steps closer to her.*) All things considered, I'm very agreeably surprised.

ANN. I'm glad.

LATHAM. (*Suddenly very serious, looks at* PETER, *turns back.*) Tell me, why are you marrying him?

ANN. I . . . (*Hesitates.*) I think what you want to know is why Peter is marrying me.

LATHAM. Well?

ANN. I know what he tells me.

LATHAM. And what is that?

ANN. (*Gathers herself.*) That he loves me and if you don't like it . . . you can— (*Realizes what she is about to say, stops short.*)

LATHAM. (*Turns to his* WIFE.) He's a real Hohenhauser. Just like your father! (*Steps Right, turns back to* ANN.) You know that he's only twenty-two.

ANN. I know.

LATHAM. He just voted for the first time. (*Looks at* PETER.) And *wrong!* (ANN *smiles.* LATHAM *goes to her.*) You realize, don't you, that you'll eventually have to live in Pittsburgh. You won't like Pittsburgh.

ANN. I haven't thought about that.

LATHAM. You'll *have* to think about it when I retire . . . and Peter takes over the company.

ANN. (*A beat.*) But, I won't have to face that for a very long time, will I? (*Looks at* PETER.)

PETER. Dad, you're just going to make a fool of yourself.

LATHAM. Well, son, I can afford to make a fool of myself. (*To* ANN.) I can afford *almost anything.* (*Crosses two steps Right.* ANN *smiles apprehensively. He goes on casually, with a smile.*) Of course, you're not interested in the subject of money . . . (*Turns his back to her.*)

ANN. Oh, yes, I am.

LATHAM. (*Turns to her, laughs.*) Ah—well, in that case—

PETER. Dad—

LATHAM. I can easily top anything you might expect from Peter—

PETER. Dad—

LATHAM. And we can all shake hands.

PETER. How about me, Dad? Who do *I* shake hands with?

LATHAM. With yourself, son. You shake hands with yourself.

ANN. (*Firmly.*) Mr. Latham . . .

LATHAM. (*Turning back to her.*) Yes, Mrs. Stanley?

ANN. I know the value of money. I wouldn't marry Peter if he didn't have some. But I'm not marrying him *for* his money. And I'm not throwing him over for *yours.*

(*They lock stares.*)

LATHAM. (*Gives her a small bow.*) Mrs. Stanley.

ANN. (*Small bow.*) Mr. Latham.

LATHAM. (*Starting up to door.*) Christine.

MRS. LATHAM. (*Small bow.*) Edgar.

LATHAM. Come along.

MRS. LATHAM. But I'm not going with you, Edgar. (*He stops.*) I *told* you. I'm going to meet Cynthia. (*He makes an impatient sound. She looks at her watch.*) And I'm a few minutes early. I'll stay on and finish this.

PETER. (*Crosses to door, puts his arm around his FATHER's shoulder.*) Come on, Dad . . . I'll buy you a drink. You need it. (*He goes, giving ANN a wink and a small wave.*)

LATHAM. (*To MRS. LATHAM.*) Your father! Just like your goddam father. (*He goes, closing the door.*)

(ANN *and* MRS. LATHAM *are left alone. They smile tentatively.*)

MRS. LATHAM. Actually, *he's* the one who's like my goddam father. Absolute bastards, both of them.

ANN. And Peter?

MRS. LATHAM. Peter's a darling. Willful, of course, but a darling. Always was. (*Smiles, pats sofa, inviting ANN to sit by her. ANN sits.*) I shall miss him very much. Boys seem to just *go away* when they grow up. He was always marvelous company. When he was little, he used to say, "When I grow up, I'm going to marry my mummy!"

(*Face to face, for a moment, then* MRS. LATHAM *turns away, realizing her gaff.*)

ANN. (*Rises, crosses Left.*) Well, there you are. I'm a dream come true!

MRS. LATHAM. It's a curse! Every time I open my mouth! (*Rises, goes to bar to fix a drink.*)

ANN. (*Sighs.*) It's the situation. It will take some getting used to. (*Starts for bar.*) Let me.

MRS. LATHAM. (*Waves her off.*) I'm going to call you Ann.

ANN. Of course.

MRS. LATHAM. And I'm Christine. You know, I find myself liking you very much. Do you golf? (*Crosses Down Right.*)

ANN. I'm afraid not.

MRS. LATHAM. (*Cheerfully. Sits in chair Right.*) Oh, well. We can always shop. Shop, shop, shop! (*Gives* ANN *a long, speculative look.*) My hunch is you'll make Peter very happy.

ANN. (*Sits on Left arm of sofa.*) Do you really think so?

MRS. LATHAM. Why shouldn't you? Youth in a woman is frightfully overrated. Look at me. When I was young, I was homely and self-conscious and shy, shy, shy! Actually, I was incapable of thinking of anything or anyone but myself. Mercifully, one grows up. One's responses to life at forty are infinitely more *tender*. Tender, tender, tender! Don't you see? You are at the very height of your—

ANN. Full sexual flowering?

MRS. LATHAM. I *like* that! (*Rises, crosses to sofa, sits.*) Shall I tell you what I really think? I think you are lucky, and I think Peter's lucky. Take me. Stuck with Edgar. Edgar, Edgar . . . (*Takes a drink.*) Oh, well. There's always golf. (*Perks up a bit.*) One must simply organize one's life *around* the Edgars. (*Looks at her watch.*) A quarter to already! It's not possible! I must run. (*Rises, puts her glass on bar.*)

(*DOORBELL rings.*)

ANN. (*Starts for door.*) Excuse me . . . (*She goes to the door and opens it. A handsome young man appears, very fashionably turned out. He is* PATRICK GRAHAM.) Yes?

PAT. Hello.

MRS. LATHAM. (*Crosses Down Right.*) Pat! Now really!

PAT. (*Goes to her.*) Christine, I've been waiting fifteen minutes. That's my *outside* limit. One could starve, starve, starve.

MRS. LATHAM. (*Laughs.*) Oh, you are spoiled.

(ANN *crosses Down Left.*)

PAT. I saw the old boy pull out, and I thought I'd come up. (*Smiles with charming intimacy at* ANN, *goes to her.*) She gets to talking and loses all sense of time.

MRS. LATHAM. (*Goes to them.*) Ann dear, I'd like to present Patrick Graham.

PAT. (*Another radiant smile.*) Hello, Ann.

(*They shake hands.*)

ANN. How do you do?

MRS. LATHAM. Patrick is one of our most promising young golfers. He was second at Pinehurst last year. I can't tell you how thrilling it was!

PAT. (*Pouting.*) But she's sending me off alone to the big Phoenix open. All by myself. (*Smiles shyly, sexily, at* ANN.) Tell her she shouldn't do that.

MRS. LATHAM. (*To* PAT.) Don't bother, pet. (*Touches his arm.*) You can't win 'em all. She's already booked. Booked, booked, booked. (*Pushes him up toward the door. Turns tranquilly to* ANN, *smiles, holds out her hand.*) Goodbye, Ann.

(*They brush cheeks. She goes to door.*)

ANN. Goodbye.

MRS. LATHAM. I'm so glad we've met.

PAT. Goodbye.

MRS. LATHAM. (*Looks at* PAT, *turns back to* ANN.) Welcome to the family.

BLACKOUT

(*FAST GYPSY MUSIC*)

ACT TWO

SCENE 4

ANN'S *apartment. A week later.*

MAUD *enters from kitchen, dressed in country tweeds. She is carrying a pot of poinsettias. She puts them on the card table, moving the ferns on the card table to the bookcase Upstage of sofa.* BILLY *is at bar, mixing a drink.*

BILLY. Maud, will you stop fooling with that shrubbery and give it to me straight?

MAUD. They're flying to Mexico tomorrow. Peter's idea. They plan to be married on Christmas Eve. *Christmas Eve!* It's sacrilegious! I wash my hands of the whole affair. (*Crosses, sits on sofa Left.*) I've done more than my share trying to fight this lunacy. Trina hasn't turned a hand, and she won't let Eddy open his mouth.

BILLY. I don't know what the hell would have been solved by letting Eddy run around with his mouth open. (*Crosses to sofa, starts to sit.*)

MAUD. And as for *you.* Nobody's ever been able to count on you. (BILLY *gets up, goes to chair Right, sits.*) I should have known you'd pick a time like this to disappear—

BILLY. I got called to the Coast. Besides, I think maybe it's better for me to stay outside it for the time being.

MAUD. That's right. The passive line has always been *your* great technique. Poor Ann.

BILLY. Maud, you haven't been my mother-in-law for a long time. How would you like a boot in the tail?

MAUD. Snarling at me isn't going to help Ann. Or *me*. Can you imagine how *I* feel? Having that nasty little boy for a son-in-law! You should see him jumping around Ann . . . devouring her with his eyes . . . It's gruesome. The boy's not normal. Thank God he didn't get his hands on Trina!

BILLY. How *about* Trina?

MAUD. Eddy is a perfect love! They're *marvelous* together. Trina leads him around by the nose. (*The DOOR-BELL rings.*) There! I guess you know who *that* is! If you don't mind, Billy, *you* can let him in. (*Rises, starts for hall.*)

· BILLY. Where do you think you're going?

MAUD. (*Stops, turns.*) To finish my packing. Trina and Eddy are taking me to the country. I shall spend Christmas as I should. With my grandchildren. (*She exits.*)

(*DOORBELL rings again.* BILLY *opens the door. It is* PETER.)

BILLY. Well, hello, young Peter!

(BILLY *closes door.* PETER's *cool through the following scene is exemplary. At* BILLY's *opening thrust,* PETER *reacts with controlled good humor.*)

PETER. Hello, old man. When did you get back?

BILLY. Glad to see me?

PETER. Ann was complaining that you'd deserted us.

BILLY. Never! I dashed back the minute my little job was finished. Well. How about offering me a drink? (*Starts Down Right.*)

PETER. (*Gives* BILLY *a curious look, but goes to bar, starts mixing a drink.*) All tuckered out?

BILLY. Not particularly, why? (*Sits sofa Right.*)

PETER. (*Shrugs; indicates the bar, where he has put himself at* BILLY's *service.*) Oh . . . you're pretty much at home around here.

BILLY. (*Smiles charmingly, indicates* PETER *himself.*) New management.

PETER. Scotch?

BILLY. Please. (PETER *pours.*) With a splash of soda. (PETER *nods, takes up a bottle, can't find an opener.*) What's the problem?

PETER. The bottle opener seems to have disappeared.

BILLY. There's an extra one that's kept in the black lacquer box on the left of the ice bucket.

PETER. (*Opens box, finds opener.*) Thanks. I'll make a note of it.

(*Holds it up triumphantly for* BILLY *to see. They smile good scouts' smile at one another.*)

BILLY. Good boy. You're a lucky guy.

PETER. Yes, I am.

(PETER *takes drink for himself, hands* BILLY *his.*)

BILLY. Oh, thank you. (*Raises the glass.*) Here's to love. (*They start to clink glasses and miss. They drink.*) Is Ann going to give up the business?

PETER. We haven't really talked about it. (*Sits in chair Right.*)

BILLY. Now that she's got somebody to take care of her. That is . . . (*Manages without words to convey the idea that* ANN *knows a good financial thing when she sees it.*) really take care of her. If you know what I mean.

PETER. (*Pleasantly.*) Yeah. I know what you mean.

BILLY. (*Drinks quietly, then tries another flank.*) I hear you're going to be married in Mexico.

PETER. That's right.

BILLY. But with no family . . . no friends around? I'd hoped to be part of the wedding party.

PETER. Really?

BILLY. Yes.

PETER. Now where did I get the impression that you were very anti the whole thing?

BILLY. I can't imagine.

PETER. You can't?

BILLY. (*Leans forward.*) Does it matter to you?

PETER. (*Leans in a bit.*) Not to *me,* no. But Ann is very fond of you.

BILLY. (*After a beat.*) You're not a bad kid.

PETER. So what is it you can't swallow?

BILLY. (*Shrugs.*) Appearances, I guess.

PETER. (*Quietly.*) Appearances.

BILLY. Next to Ann—now, don't get me wrong, fella—but next to Ann, you don't appear to be . . . completely . . . mature . . . (*Makes hand gesture indicating baby.*)

PETER. (*Smiles.*) Whereas you do. Shows you how appearances can be deceiving.

(BILLY *gets up.* PETER *rises. They stare at each other for a moment.* ANN *comes out of her room. Her hair and dress more youthful than we have seen it before.*)

ANN. (*Goes to* BILLY. *They embrace.*) Billy! Why didn't someone tell me you were here? Oh, I'm so glad you got back! Did Peter tell you we're leaving tomorrow?

(*She holds* BILLY's *hand, then takes* PETER's *hand.* BILLY *looks at her.*)

BILLY. Yes. He told me. You look . . . (*Rather taken aback.*) Well wowareenie!

ANN. I'm switched on for the Electric Circus.

BILLY. New hair-do.

ANN. Kenneth. Peter says any woman who can't spend a hundred dollars a week on her hair and face and fingertips isn't *trying.*

BILLY. Is *that* what Peter says?

PETER. Uh-huh.

ANN. Do you like?

BILLY. I like. (*A gentle smile.*) I always liked. (*He pulls* ANN *to him. She pulls her hand away.*)

ANN. (*Glorying in this tacit rivalry between the* TWO MEN.) Ah! *Now* you tell me. Well, it's too late. I am . . . (*Smiles tenderly at* PETER.) bespoke. (*Turns back to* BILLY *with a look of happy malice.*) Oh, say, I saw Elke Schnitzel in the elevator yesterday. Her nose was running.

BILLY. Now, don't knock my bit of holiday cheer. Her boss is leaving, and Elke and I have the place to ourselves. But enough of me. Where are you headed in that extravaganza?

ANN. We're going to Max's Kansas City for dinner, then to Cafe La Mama, then to the Electric Circus. Then, maybe later to the Graffiti. Who knows? The night's before us.

BILLY. (*To* ANN.) How things have changed! (*To* PETER.) I can't ever remember being able to keep Ann out past eleven-thirty.

ANN. Well, now I love it! Don't I, Peter?

PETER. She loves it.

BILLY. She loves it. (*Crosses to sofa, hitting side of head as if to unstop his ear, sits.*) I went to the Electric Circus once. Just *once.*

ANN. (*Crossing Upstage sofa to Left.*) If you think I'm going to be scared off by a little noise! Hey, Billy! Wait till you see us zooming around town on the new Triumph Trophy Two-Five-Oh!

BILLY. The new what?

PETER. It's a bike.

ANN. A *motorcycle.* Peter just bought it. (*Proudly.*) We got arrested last week! Oh, Billy, it was wild! (*Sits on Left arm of sofa, a la motorcycle.*) We were pulled up waiting for a light at Third and Seventieth, and this black leather-jacket va-va-varoomed up beside us and said, "Whaddaya get outa the tricycle, Louise?" "Lew-eeze!" He couldn't have been more offensive! So I said, "If you can get somebody to help you tow that junk heap over to the Drive, we'll see who can get what!" So he gunned after us— (*Makes motorcycle noise.*) and we got on the Drive and he never came close to us! Unfortunately, at

Ninety-Sixth Street there was this cop. (*Makes motor-cycle noise.*) *He* came close to us. (ANN *and* PETER *laugh.*)

BILLY. (*A long beat as he regards her, then turns quietly to* PETER.) Another Scotch. Deep dish.

PETER. Yes, sir. (*Takes glass, goes to bar.*)

(TRINA *opens front door, she and* EDDY *appear.*)

TRINA. Hi.

EDDY. Hi, everybody.

ANN. Hi!

(MAUD *surges into the room from hall, ready to leave, an overnight bag in hand.*)

MAUD. You didn't have to come up, darlings. I could easily have met you downstairs.

TRINA. (*Crosses Down Center to* ANN, *followed by* EDDY.) I wanted to see Mummy before she leaves.

(ANN *goes to meet her. They embrace.*)

ANN. Hello, darling. (*Crosses to* EDDY.) Hello, Eddy.

EDDY. (*Hesitates a moment, starts to shake her hand.*) Mother. (*Chuckles, then kisses her on cheek.*)

ANN. Have you time for a drink?

EDDY. I think maybe we'd better not—the roads are going to be crowded as hell.

ANN. Oh, dear . . . I always hate it when I know Trina is out in holiday traffic—

BILLY. At least *Trina* is in a *car.* (*He makes motor-cycle noise.*)

TRINA. Oh, Mummy, may I have a word with you?

ANN. Will you excuse us?

(*She follows* TRINA *into her bedroom.* PETER *crosses Down Right.*)

MAUD. (*To* EDDY, *Upstage of sofa.*) I want to stop and pick up some tree ornaments. There never are enough . . .

EDDY. (*Goes to bar.*) Okay. You may be right. I thought I'd about bought out the store, but that tree's ten feet tall. (*To* BILLY.) I told them to send the biggest one they had.

(BILLY *smiles.*)

MAUD. If only it will snow. We can go to midnight mass at the little church in the village. (*To* BILLY.) Billy, Eddy got truffles for the turkey dressing.

PETER. Truffles!

EDDY. (*Crossing to* PETER.) It's a twenty-pounder! I told them to get the biggest one they had. (*Turns to* BILLY.) Who're you spending Christmas with, Billy boy?

BILLY. As luck would have it, I'm having Christmas right here in the building. I'm sharing my loneliness with another—single.

EDDY. (*To* PETER.) I'll bet it's a big blond single.

BILLY. I told them to get the biggest one they had!

(*They laugh.*)

MAUD. You're going to be here in the building? Then would you do me a little favor, Billy dear? Would you be kind enough to stop in and water my ferns?

BILLY. Ferns?

MAUD. (*Hands key to* BILLY.) I was madly worried about the ferns. Now, not too *much* water.

BILLY. Just a splash. The way I take it. (*To* EDDY.) Say, Ed, when is the big day for you and Trina?

EDDY. I wanted Trina to finish high school . . . (*Hesitates.*) But—uh— (*Laughs.*) She doesn't want to wait. So I guess we're gonna get the job done pretty soon.

MAUD. (*Firmly.*) Not until the *clothes* we've ordered are ready. I insisted that Trina have a proper trousseau.

EDDY. So I've got to wait for word from Paraphernalia, whatever the hell *that* is.

(ANN *and* TRINA *return.*)

TRINA. Are you ready, Granny Maud?

EDDY. (*Grabbing bag and going to door.*) We're off, folks!

(PETER *drifts up to desk.*)

TRINA. Goodbye, Mummy. I hope you'll be happy. I really do.

ANN. (*We see that she is moved.*) Oh, Trina! (*Kisses her.*)

TRINA. (*Goes to* BILLY.) Merry Christmas, Bi'ly. (*Kisses* BILLY, *turns to* PETER.) You'd better be good to my mother. (*Goes to door.*)

EDDY. All the best, Ann.

ANN. To you too, Eddy.

MAUD. (*Going to* BILLY.) *Joyeux Noel,* Billy dear. (*Gives him a peck. Crosses to* ANN.) Merry Christmas, Ann.

(*They kiss.*)

ANN. Merry Christmas, Mother.

MAUD. (*Passes* PETER *on way to door.*) *Hohenhouser!*

(*She goes, followed by* TRINA *and* EDDY. *He closes the door.*)

BILLY. (*Gets up.*) Well, I guess I'll follow the general movement—

ANN. No. Stay. Please. (*Crosses to Center.*)

BILLY. What's the matter?

(PETER *crosses Down Right.*)

ANN. Trina is pregnant.

BILLY. Oh? (*To* PETER.) Now she'll never finish high school. (*To* ANN.) Is she terribly upset?

ANN. She? *Me!*

PETER. Forget it, Ann.

ANN. Forget it? She's only seventeen. And she's my daughter. My only child. And I'm— (*A thought.*) Oh, I'm going to be a grandmother!

BILLY. (*To* PETER.) I guess we know what that makes you. (*Hands him a cigar.*) Have a cigar.

PETER. Come on, Ann. We were going out, so let's go out.

ANN. Poor little Trina.

PETER. Poor little Trina! She could have kept the big news until after our wedding.

ANN. Oh, Peter—

BILLY. I'm forced to agree with young Peter.

ANN. (*Gives a shaky little laugh.*) You've got to admit my cup runneth over.

BILLY. You're the sexiest grandmother in my crowd.

ANN. Thank you for being here tonight, Billy.

BILLY. Oh, I'm *always* here. Don't you know that? You know, I've just figured out what it is that's been bugging me all evening . . . I'm jealous. (*He goes.*)

PETER. (*When* BILLY *is gone.*) He meant it, you know, what he said. He *is* jealous. And he's surprised that he is.

ANN. He's just that perverse! He was never jealous when we were married.

PETER. I am . . . extremely jealous of him. I feel very threatened by Billy.

ANN. Well, you needn't. You're terribly possessive, you know.

PETER. I know. Every time I see you even shake hands with another guy, I get a big blast of the old territorial imperative.

ANN. I can never believe it will last—

PETER. It will last as long as you want it. I'll be here as long as you'll have me.

ANN. *Why?*

PETER. Because you're very neat with Kleenex.

ANN. (*Steps Right to him.*) Peter. I do wish I'd known you sooner.

(*They embrace.*)

PETER. I like now.

ANN. Oh, I like now, too. Do you know that for the first time in my life I can really *count* on someone else? And a little child shall lead her . . .

PETER. (*Steps back.*) Ann, I swear to God, if you make one more joke about my age—

ANN. Shut up. I'm older than you! (*She kisses him.*)

PETER. Let's skip the Electric Circus. (*Embraces her.*)

ANN. Not on your life! I'm already plugged in. (*She does a dance step.*)

BLACKOUT

(ROCK 'N' ROLL MUSIC)

(STROBES START FLASHING)

ACT TWO

SCENE 5

ANN's *apartment. The same evening, around midnight.*

After a moment, the front door opens. ANN *and* PETER *enter. He turns on the LIGHTS. She removes coat and tosses it on chair Right.*

ANN. (*Crosses Down Right.*) Oh, my God! How can you stand it!

PETER. (*Crosses Right to sofa.*) It's just a joint. It's okay.

ANN. *Okay?* It's an *assault!* That kind of bombardment could break down your chromosomes. How can you take it? (*Goes into kitchen.*)

PETER. (*Sits on Right arm of sofa.*) It's just a joint!

ANN. (*Comes out of kitchen with bottle of Alka Seltzer, crosses Upstage sofa to bar.*) You knew everybody in there! Every single solitary living whatever-theywere! Who was that girl dressed in Saran-Wrap? (*Picks up glass of water at bar, puts three Alka Seltzer tablets in it.*)

PETER. Polly.

ANN. Oh. Polly. And that gloomy Botticelli who sat on you for half the evening? I failed to catch her name. If it was offered . . .

PETER. Gabriella . . . she's a nice kid . . . a little kinkie . . . but nice.

ANN. You seemed to know her well.

PETER. Sure, I know her.

ANN. Is there something between you?

PETER. No.

ANN. Never?

PETER. Not really.

ANN. But you've slept with her?

PETER. A couple of times.

ANN. (*Crosses Down Left.*) She's the most beautiful girl I've ever seen.

PETER. (*Indifferently.*) Yeah, she's a beauty, all right.

ANN. What's the matter with you? She's breathtaking! How old is she?·Eighteen? And you let something like that get away from you?

PETER. (*Rises, speaks gently.*) What's the matter, Ann?

ANN. Nothing! It's just that that place got on my nerves. The environment was so animated and the inhabitants so inert! (*Sits on sofa Left.*)

PETER. That's their style.

ANN. I dare say. (*Sighs.*) I'm sorry, Peter. It was all a big mistake. We should have gone to . . . Radio City and Rumpelmayer's.

PETER. We'll be out of here tomorrow afternoon. Relax. (*Sits next to her on sofa.*)

ANN. Thank goodness I've finished packing. I have a fantastically aching head. (*She leans back on his arm.*)

PETER. Come on. Relax a little.

ANN. No . . . it's late. (*They get up.*) I'd rather you went on home, Peter. I'm absolutely done in. I'll just finish this Alka Seltzer and go to bed.

PETER. (*Going to her.*) All right.

ANN. Don't be angry with me, Peter.

PETER. I'm not. But if I don't go right now, I won't go at all. Okay? (*Gives her a tender but brief kiss.*)

ANN. Thank you, darling.

PETER. (*Crosses to door.*) I'll pick you up around eleven-thirty.

ANN. I'll be waiting.

PETER. Get some sleep now.

ANN. Oh, God, I just remembered. Mother snatched my last sleeping pill.

PETER. You sure you—?

ANN. Oh, well, maybe the Alka Seltzer will do it.

PETER. Sure you don't want me to stay? I'll massage your neck . . . You're all tensed up . . .

ANN. (*Crosses two steps Upstage.*) I just want to crawl into bed and black out.

PETER. (*A beat.*) Okay. Eleven-thirty.

ANN. Eleven-thirty.

(*He goes.* ANN *goes to bar, picks up bottle of Alka Seltzer, sips from her glass, starts Down Right for her room, picking up her jacket and purse, and putting out LIGHT in the room. The bedroom door opens and* BILLY *appears. She backs into the living room. He is in his shirtsleeves, tie off, drink and cigar in hand.*)

BILLY. (*Hoarse whisper.*) It's the Ghost of Christmas Past. (*Goes past her.*)

ANN. (*At bedroom door.*) What are you doing here? Who let you in?

BILLY. (*Same whisper.*) Maud gave me her key. (*Crosses Left three steps.*) To take care of the ferns.

ANN. Humbug! They don't need taking care of at this hour. They need their sleep.

BILLY. (*Turns.*) Elke's still busy. And I knew you weren't here, so I just dropped in to look at your TV. When Elke finishes—

ANN. The TV is in *here*. What the devil are you doing in my bedroom?

BILLY. I ducked out when I heard you coming. I didn't want to compromise you.

ANN. You've been standing behind that door with your fat ear pasted to the keyhole!

BILLY. It was hardly necessary. (*A beat.*) If I were you, Ann, I wouldn't torture myself going on and on and on about all the pretty girls Peter—

ANN. Oh, stop it, Billy. Finish your drink. And fix me one. (*Turns LIGHTS back on.*)

BILLY. I thought you wanted me to go.

(*She goes into bedroom.*)

ANN'S VOICE. (*Offstage.*) Fix me a drink.

(*He goes to bar. She leaves the door open while* BILLY *fixes her drink and refills his own. He raises his voice so she can hear him.*)

BILLY. I've been waiting for a chance to tell you *my* news.

ANN'S VOICE. What is it?

BILLY. I've had a break. I'm not going to be at the mercy of my future son-in-law for a handout.

ANN'S VOICE. Your *what?*

BILLY. My *ex*-future son-in-law? My future ex-son-in-law? You know, Eddy. *Anyway.* What I was *trying* to say, I was at this party and ran into Benjamin Wittenberg.

ANN'S VOICE. Who?

BILLY. Benjamin Wittenberg . . . the big public rela-
tions guy. His clients are real biggies, like General Motors,
AT&T, Raquel Welch, New Zealand . . . (*Crosses Down
Right, sits on arm of chair.*) Well, we got to talking—and
I told him how I'd been feeling lately, you know, about
makeup and elevator shoes . . . Well, he picked it up
fast. "You're right, Boylan," he said. He said, "Boylan,
I'm not knocking your profession, but when a man reaches
forty, he wants to be in the mainstream of American life."
So, he sent me up to see a client of his. Federico Orsini.

ANN'S VOICE. (*Offstage.*) The Italian?

BILLY. What else! Biggest film producer in Italy . . .
makes dirty Westerns . . . uses a lot of American people
. . . and they want someone to handle the American and
English press. I'd be joining their office in Rome.

ANN. (*Entering from bedroom, dressed in robe and
slippers.*) Rome? You're going to enter the mainstream of
American life by way of Rome?

BILLY. (*Hands her a drink, rises, crosses to Left
Center.*) I thought you'd be pleased for me.

ANN. You are abandoning me.

BILLY. Who's getting married, you or me?

ANN. It's times like this when a person needs friends
and support and . . . and affection—

BILLY. You have young Peter for affection.

ANN. It isn't the same thing! You were my husband
first!

BILLY. (*Steps Right.*) Be that as it may, I don't see
myself in the role of inseparable friend to the newlyweds.
What's eating you, Annie? Still have some doubts about
tomorrow?

ANN. *No.*

BILLY. Then you're okay.

ANN. (*Sits chair Right.*) It's more complicated than
that.

BILLY. Ah.

ANN. He's . . . he's so touching, Billy . . . the way

he tries to make everything easy for me. And he's so damn young. He should be thinking about himself all the time. But he doesn't. He's so considerate and so sensitive to what *I* want . . . what's right for *me*. (*Pauses*.) Who's worrying about what's right for *him?* Oh, Billy, when I stand back and look at him, I can't help seeing how attractive he is. It was a very bad idea to go to the Electric Circus.

BILLY. (*Sits sofa Right*.) I know what you mean. When you see a whole bunch of them together . . . (*Puffs on cigar*.)

ANN. He deserves something more than—

BILLY. Annie, are you absolutely *sure* you're not in love with him?

ANN. I love . . . his being in love with me. Would you give me a little more Scotch?

BILLY. If you drink any more, you won't sleep.

ANN. (*Rises, crosses to bar*.) Why don't we just get smashed. Together. How about it?

BILLY. Well, why not? It's my birthday. Thirty-ei . . . Forty-three.

ANN. (*Crosses to him*.) Today's the twenty-second! I'm sorry, darling!

BILLY. Don't be sorry. I thought you were displaying the most exquisite tact. I've stopped looking forward to these little milestones.

ANN. (*Upstage sofa*.) Oh, Billy! Thank you for being forty-three. I can't tell you how grateful I am! (*Hugs him*.) Happy birthday, darling! (*DOORBELL rings*.) It's the doorbell.

BILLY. Yes, it is. It certainly is. (*Puts cigar in ashtray on coffee table*.).

ANN. Who on earth—?

BILLY. (*Gets up*.) It's *Elke!*

ANN. Elke?

BILLY. I didn't think she'd come down here. She doesn't approve of you. (*Goes towards bedroom*.)

ANN. Of me! *She* disapproves of *me!* Billy—where are you going?

BILLY. (*At bedroom door.*) If she finds me here, with *you*, I've had it. Get rid of her. Tell her I was gone when you came home. Act indignant.

ANN. I *am* indignant!

BILLY. Splendid! Use the Method!

(*DOORBELL rings again.* BILLY *shuts bedroom door.* ANN *sees the cigar which is smoking in the ashtray. She picks the cigar up, puffs vigorously until it's smoking heavily and puts it down in full view, where it cannot be missed, grins, and then with a determined air, goes to the door and opens it.* PETER *stands on the threshold.* ANN *catches her breath.*)

ANN. Oh. You're not Elke! I thought you were—

PETER. (*Hands her a small bottle.*) I was worried you couldn't sleep. I had to go to a couple of guys . . . but I finally found some.

ANN. Oh, Peter, that wasn't necessary . . . I . . .

PETER. I thought you'd be in bed—

ANN. No . . . I mean I haven't—

PETER. You look all flushed. What's the matter? You don't have a fever, do you? (*Puts out his hand to her forehead.*)

ANN. (*She moves back from him.*) No! I'm all right. I'm . . . just surprised to see you . . .

(PETER *suddenly is conscious of the cigar smoke. He looks curiously around, spots it, crosses down to coffee table, picks up cigar, looks at bedroom door, stubs out cigar and heads for front door.*)

PETER. (*Very cold.*) I . . . guess I made a mistake . . . coming back unexpectedly.

ANN. No, no—

PETER. Sorry I barged in. I should have known better.
Good night, Ann. (PETER *closes the door*.)

ANN. Peter! Wait a minute . . . Oh, Peter, let me
exp—

(*He is gone. She stands frozen staring at the door. After
a moment,* BILLY *sticks his head out*.)

BILLY. All cleared away?

ANN. (*Quietly*.) You might say that. (*Suddenly whirls
on him*.) Get out of here! (*She crosses Down Left to
Center*.) Go pollute somebody else's air for a change!
You bastard! You swine! *You goddam actor!*

BILLY. (*Who has been trying to stop this assault*.)
What did I do?

ANN. He saw your cigar and went storming out of here!
(*Starts to cry*.) Billy, I've begged you for years to give
up smoking! (*Slumps over on sofa*.)

BLACKOUT

(*FAST GYPSY MUSIC*)

ACT TWO

SCENE 6

ANN'S *apartment. Late morning, the next day. The cur-
tains are open. Full SUNSHINE streams in.*

ANN *paces Right and* MRS. MARGOLIN *is seated on Right
arm of sofa.*

MRS. MARGOLIN. Two words would clear it all up. You
know that.

ANN. Can't you just hear me trying to justify my ex-husband's presence to a twenty— (*Takes a deep breath.*) to Peter? You should have seen him. Clenched teeth, narrowed eyes! It was too ridiculous . . . too humiliating.

MRS. MARGOLIN. Humiliation is as humiliation does.

ANN. What does that mean? (*Sits chair Right.*)

MRS. MARGOLIN. I don't know. Call him.

ANN. No. I really don't want to talk to him. I wrote him a letter. Billy took it to him this morning.

MRS. MARGOLIN. A letter? He'll die.

ANN. He's twenty-two. He'll live.

MRS. MARGOLIN. But will you? (*Starting off.*) Well, somebody's got to look after the store.

ANN. I'll be there this afternoon.

MRS. MARGOLIN. Just what you need. Call him.

ANN. Margy, give up. Give up on me.

MRS. MARGOLIN. (*At door.*) Never! Never! There's got to be somebody.

(BILLY *opens the door, enters.*)

BILLY. Hi, Margy.

MRS. MARGOLIN. (*To* ANN.) Anybody but him. (*She goes.*)

BILLY. (*Crossing Down Left.*) How is everything?

ANN. (*Falsely bright.*) Fine! (*Rises.*) How about lunch? Something special. Let's go spend lots of money. You can start getting the feel of the expense account lunch.

BILLY. Great! Get your coat . . .

ANN. (*Starts Right.*) And, Billy . . . (*She stops.*) Now that it's all over . . .

BILLY. (*When she doesn't go on.*) What is it, kid?

ANN. (*Quietly.*) I've done the right thing, haven't I?

BILLY. You've done the right thing.

ANN. (*She starts to go again.*) It was impossible, wasn't it? (*Stops.*)

BILLY. Absolutely. Get your coat.

(ANN *goes into bedroom.* PETER *comes in front door. He*

and BILLY *look at each other deadpan for a moment.*
ANN *re-enters with coat and bag.)*

ANN. Let's go to that new— (*Staring at* PETER, *stunned.*) Hello, Peter.
PETER. (*At door.*) Hello, Ann.
ANN. How are you?
PETER. I'm all right.
ANN. What are you doing here?
PETER. Our plane leaves in an hour.
ANN. Oh.
PETER. (*Comes down to* ANN.) Look, Ann, I spent the whole night kicking myself . . . and then I went over to Billy's place and let him kick me . . . and well, here I am. So, say goodbye while I get your bags.

(*He puts her coat and bag on chair Right, pushes her Left toward* BILLY. *He starts for the bedroom.*)

ANN. But—
BILLY. (*Grabs her shoulders.*) Behave.

(PETER *has disappeared into bedroom.*)

ANN. You knew he was coming here.
BILLY. We rode over together.
ANN. Didn't you give him my letter?
BILLY. Letter? Oh, the letter. What the hell did I do with that . . . (*Starts searching his pockets.*)
ANN. But, Billy—

(PETER *comes out with two cases, sets them down.*)

PETER. I'll get the rest of them. (*Starts back for bedroom.*)
ANN. Peter . . .

(BILLY *clutches the back of her hair.*)

PETER. (*Turns back.*) What is it?

ANN. There's . . . I forgot my toothbrush.

PETER. (*Goes off.*) I'll get it.

ANN. (*Calling after him.*) And my Blush-On. Don't forget my Blush-On.

PETER. (*Offstage.*) Blush-On?

ANN. It's in the—

BILLY. Second drawer on the left.

ANN. *Why*, Billy? You were so against it.

BILLY. (*Shrugs.*) Do you know how many "B" pictures I've made?

(*They embrace.*)

ANN. It's a gigantic mistake.

BILLY. (*Solemnly.*) It has been obvious to me for some time that that is what God put us here for. To make gigantic mistakes. It is His Supreme Design.

(PETER *re-enters with two more bags.*)

PETER. (*Crosses to her.*) Is this all?

ANN. I think so.

PETER. (*Shakes* BILLY's *hand.*) Thanks, Billy.

BILLY. Beat it.

PETER. (*Starting off.*) I'll ring for the elevator— (*Pointing to bags on floor.*) and come back for those two.

BILLY. I'll get them.

(PETER *goes.* BILLY *gets* ANN's *coat, puts it on her. He takes out letter from his pocket, slowly tears it into small pieces and puts them into* ANN's *hand.*)

ANN. Thanks, Billy.

BILLY. I've finally decided that you're grownup enough to marry the kid.

ANN. Goodbye, Billy. (*He embraces her, suddenly lets her go, picks up bags.*) Billy . . . (*Steps towards* BILLY.)

PETER. (*He reappears in the doorway.*) The elevator's here. Come on, love.

(*GREEK MUSIC SOFTLY UNDER*)

BILLY. Go on, hold it. I got these. (PETER *disappears.* BILLY *goes for the bags, starts for the door.*) Come on, Ann.

(ANN *is just standing there.* BILLY, *at door, stops and looks at her.*)

ANN. Oh, dear . . .
BILLY. What's the matter?
ANN. I was just wondering how Helen of Troy managed about her ex-husband.
BILLY. He was an older guy, you know. They let him take care of the luggage. (*He goes.*)

(ANN, *left alone, looks around the room, crosses up to door, and then looks down at the torn letter in her hand and flings the pieces into the air as though they were rice or confetti. She flings them so they come down around her head.*)

ANN. (*Tentatively, trying the sound of it.*) Here comes the bride. (*Catches her breath.*) Oh, God! (*She goes.*)

CURTAIN

(*MUSIC SWELLS*)

FURNITURE, SET AND HAND PROPS
FOR PRESET

ACT ONE

GREEK SET:
  Motorcycle
  2 tables
  3 chairs
In Cafe:
  Telephone
  Bottle ouzo with shot glass on top (set on coffee table-apt)
  On Table Left:
    1 shot glass
  On Table Right:
    Straw hat between table leg and chair
    Crumpled tissues
  Right of Table Right:
    Straw Bag With:
      Box man-size Kleenex
      Roll Baggies large
      Rubberbands
      Plastic glass
PRESET ON OFFICE FLYING UNIT:
  Magazine on Left of bench
OFFICE SET:
  Small bookshelf Right with telephone
  Large chair Upstage of it
  Filing Cabinets With:
    Top drawer extreme Left partially filled with folders and
      sets of keys
    Top drawer second from Left completely filled with folders
  1 small chair Right of desk
  1 large chair Left of desk
  Desk With:
    Typewriter with paper already in
    Telephone Left of Typewriter
    Pencil well with sharpened pencils
    Files Right of Typewriter
    Paper
    Blueprint
    Long list of apartments
    Mrs. Adams' purse and gloves

On Coat Hooks:
　　Ann's coat and scarf
　　Margolin's coat and purse
In Dressing Room Right:
　　Files
　　Large vitabeth empty
　　Hand towel

APARTMENT SET:
　Sofa With:
　　4 throw pillows (2 pink—2 brown)
　　1 magazine
　Armchair Right with 1 throw pillow (light brown)
　End Table Left of Armchair With:
　　Ashtray
　　Cigarette holder with cigarettes
　End Table Left of Sofa With:
　　Ashtray with little water
　Coffee Table With:
　　Ashtray
　　Cigarette lighter
　　Cigarette holder with cigarettes (extreme Left on table)
　Console Table With:
　　Radio (extreme Right of table)
　　Lamp
　Leaf Table Left With:
　　Bowl of leaves
　　Deck of cards
　　Scorepad
　　Pencil
2 chairs either end of leaf table

Desk Up Right With:
　　Telephone in Down Left corner
　　Picture of Ann
　　Ashtray
　　Cigarette lighter
　　Lamp
　On Handrail:
　　Trina's raincoat and purse
　Table with lamp outside front door
　Leaf flowers in window boxes

In Kitchen:
   Tray with 6 old-fashioned glasses and apple
   Apron for Boylan change
   1 full bottle of Alka-Seltzer
   Pill bottle
   Television set—antenna up
On Bar:
   Black box with church key
   Ice bucket with ice
   Water pitcher with fresh water
   Ouzo bottle
   2 decanters
   1 bottle bourbon with pourer
   1 bottle Scotch with pourer
   Tray with 6 old-fashioned glasses
   Extra glasses under bar (10)

PROP TABLE

PETER:
   Marrons glaces
   4 suitcases
   Paper money

BILLY:
   Letters (rigged)
   Highball glass half-filled with Scotch
   Large bag with Chinese food
   Extra box cigars
   Extra cigar tips—glass holder for cigar
   1 cigar unwrapped with tip on end

TRINA:
   Loose leaf and cram books
   Needlepoint
   Sunglasses

MAUD:
   Umbrella
   Key for front door
   Overnight bag

ANN:
   Key for front door

PROP DEPARTMENT

Bottle Perrier
Ann's glass
Extra old-fashioned glasses
Poinsettia plant (for Maud)
Large flower plant (for Maud)
4 small azalea plants
Wreath
Extra ashtray
Fabric swatches
Billy's plaid jacket (from dresser)

PERSONAL PROPS

PETER:
  Lighter
  Paper money
  Watch

BILLY:
  Cigars
  Tips
  Watch
  Lighter
  Letters

ANN:
  Eyeglasses
  Sunglasses

TRINA:
  Sunglasses

MRS. LATHAM:
  Watch

ACT ONE—MOVES

AFTER GREEK SCENE—Take straw basket, hat, ouzo from actors
Down Right. Then set coffee table on pivot to mark

AFTER OFFICE SCENE—Turn Left chair into table and straighten
office. Strike magazine

AFTER APARTMENT SCENE—Strike magazine, clear glass off bar, straighten pillows

AFTER OFFICE SCENE—Straighten office

AFTER APARTMENT SCENE—Enter from bedroom and set Billy's plaid jacket on armchair Right

 During this scene have large flower plant ready for Maud

AFTER APARTMENT SCENE—Nothing

INTERMISSION

Reset bar adding Perrier bottle with top and Ann's glass

Replace ashtray on sofa end table

Reset bowl on leaf table and strike flower plant

Strike marrons glaces from coffee table

Place leaf down and straighten chairs

Change leaf flowers to azalas in window boxes

Clear drink glasses

Clean ashtrays

Straighten pillows

Set large fabric book on leaf table Right of bowl

Set small fabric book on coffee table Up Left corner

Set 3 large fabric materials over sofa back

Strike television

ACT TWO—MOVES

AFTER APARTMENT SCENE—Strike all fabric swatches. Clear drink glass at bar. Straighten pillows

AFTER OFFICE SCENE—Immediately strike bookcase and chair Upstage

AFTER APARTMENT SCENE—When actors clear front door set wreath

AFTER APARTMENT SCENE—No change

DURING APARTMENT SCENE—Set highball glass half filled on office table. Strike Alka-Seltzer and Ann's glass

AFTER APARTMENT SCENE—Enter from Down Right and strike cigar on coffee table. Strike ashtray on coffee table. Strike bolt from coffee table. Strike as many drink glasses as possible from end table, armchair and bar.

 Immediately following this change set suitcases outside of bedroom door. Check dresser with Ann's coat and bag

AFTER SECOND ACT CURTAIN—Strike coffee table for curtain calls

COSTUME PLOT

ACT ONE

SCENE ONE:

    ANN—Light sleeveless summer dress, straw hat, sandals, large straw handbag

    PETER—T-shirt, khaki pants, sandals

SCENE TWO:

    ANN—Smart crisp office suit, white blouse, flat shoes, black handbag, white gloves, etc.

    MRS. MARGOLIN—Beige wool office dress, simple and efficient

    BILLY—Very dapper double-breasted blue lounge suit, shirt, tie, etc.

    MRS. ADAMS—Smart grey and white suit, grey hat

    EDDY—Grey suit, faintly western, short alligator boots

SCENE THREE:

    MAUD—Sedate black dress, very bright red tights, noticeable pearl earrings, black shoes

    TRINA—Grey miniskirt, white blouse, off-white boots, yellow coat, beige purse

    PETER—Light tan sports jacket, grey slacks, white turtleneck, loafers

    ANN—Blue and white dressing gown, mules. Underdress new costume for next scene

SCENE FOUR:

    ANN—New grey office dress, trench coat, black bag, etc.

    MAUD—Plastic flowered raincoat, umbrella, black shoes

    PETER—Jacket and slacks of I-3, blue shirt

    MRS. MARGOLIN—Navy blue dress, trench coat, bag

SCENE FIVE:

    MAUD—Black dress as I-3, pearls, etc.

    PETER—Same as I-4

    TRINA—Camel's hair miniskirt and sweater, brown boots

ANN—Beautiful short dinner dress, evening bag, gloves

EDDY—Dark dressed-up suit, white shirt, tie, etc.

BILLY—Double-breasted blue blazer, grey slacks, shirt, tie

SCENE SIX:

TRINA—Add yellow trench coat to I-5 costume (very quick)

BILLY—Same I-5. Perhaps darker plaid sports jacket for later in scene. Apron

ANN—Black lounging pajamas, flat shoes (very quick change)

PETER—Very good looking double-breasted blue blazer, slacks, shirt, tie, loafers

MAUD—(coming from movie) Brown coat and leopard hat

SCENE SEVEN:

MAUD—(Very quick change) Sedate pastel housecoat over dress

TRINA—At home chino slacks, orange sweater, black shoes

PETER—Very good looking dark pin striped suit, shirt, tie

ANN—New red office dress, coat, bag. (This is one month later)

ACT TWO

SCENE ONE:

ANN—Lovely pink kaftan housecoat or hostess gown. She must underdress blouse and skirt for next office scene, a very quick change

EDDY—Dark olive three piece suit

TRINA—Yellow sweater, corduroy pants, black flat shoes

MAUD—Beige dress

SCENE TWO:

BILLY—Glen plaid three piece suit

MRS. MARGOLIN—dark grey office dress, trench coat, bag

ANN—Mauve blouse and lavender skirt (previously underdressed)

SCENE THREE:

ANN—Add lavender jacket to II-2 costume (very quick)

PETER—Another darkish suit, business-like-Madison Avenue

MRS. LATHAM—Elegant blue dress, full length tourmaline mink coat, shoes, bag, etc.

MR. LATHAM—Dark three piece pin-stripe suit, hat in hand

PAT—Double-breasted grey plaid suit

SCENE FOUR:

MAUD—Beige and grey dress, beige jacket, change to brown coat

BILLY—Three piece grey pin stripe suit

PETER—Double breasted blue blazer, white turtleneck, grey slacks

ANN—Charming short white turtleneck dress, double-breasted blue blazer

TRINA—Red and blue plaid suit, blue tights, red scarf, blue boots

EDDY—Sports jacket and ascot

SCENE FIVE:

PETER—Same as II-4, add trench coat

ANN—Same as II-4, add blue bag. She changes to blue and white dressing gown—underdresses next costume

BILLY—Loose jacket

SCENE SIX:

MRS. MARGOLIN—Trench coat, scarf and bag

ANN—Grey wool dress (I-4), tweed traveling coat, black bag

BILLY—Topcoat (black and white checked) over grey suit of II-4

PETER—Trench coat and scarf over costume of II-4

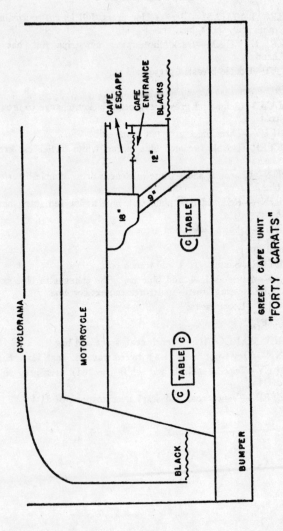

GREEK CAFE UNIT
"FORTY CARATS"

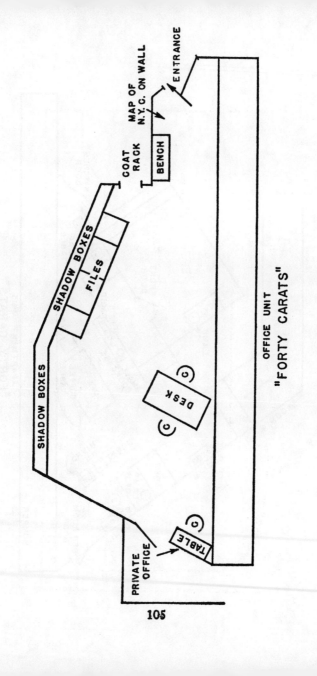

ENTRANCE

MAP OF
N.Y.C. ON WALL

COAT
RACK

BENCH

SHADOW BOXES

FILES

SHADOW BOXES

DESK

PRIVATE
OFFICE

TABLE

OFFICE UNIT
"FORTY CARATS"

105

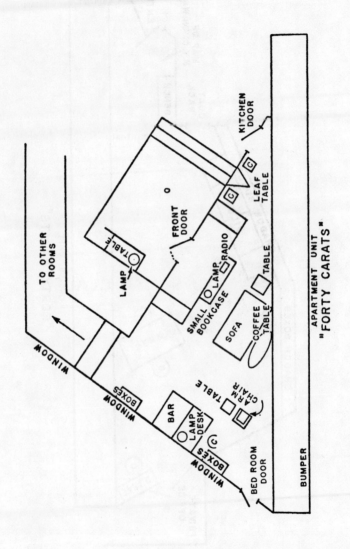

APARTMENT UNIT
"FORTY CARATS"

106

6 RMS RIV VU
BOB RANDALL
(Little Theatre) Comedy
4 Men, 4 Women, Interior

A vacant apartment with a river view is open for inspection by prospective tenants, and among them are a man and a woman who have never met before. They are the last to leave and, when they get ready to depart, they find that the door is locked and they are shut in. Since they are attractive young people, they find each other interesting and the fact that both are happily married adds to their delight of mutual, yet obviously separate interests.

> ". . . a Broadway comedy of fun and class, as cheerful as a rising soufflé. A sprightly, happy comedy of charm and humor. Two people playing out a very vital game of love, an attractive fantasy with a precious tincture of truth to it."—*N.Y. Times.* ". . . perfectly charming entertainment, sexy, romantic and funny."—*Women's Wear Daily.*

Royalty, $50—$35

WHO KILLED SANTA CLAUS?
TERENCE FEELY
(All Groups) Thriller
6 Men, 2 Women, Interior

Barbara Love is a popular television 'auntie'. It is Christmas, and a number of men connected with her are coming to a party. Her secretary, Connie, is also there. Before they arrive she is threatened by a disguised voice on her Ansaphone, and is sent a grotesque 'murdered' doll in a coffin, wearing a dress resembling one of her own. She calls the police, and a handsome detective arrives. Shortly afterwards her guests follow. It becomes apparent that one of those guests is planning to kill her. Or is it the strange young man who turns up unexpectedly, claiming to belong to the publicity department, but unknown to any of the others?

> ". . . is a thriller with heaps of suspense, surprises, and nattily cleaver turns and twists . . . Mr. Feeley is technically highly skilled in the artificial range of operations, and his dialogue is brilliantly effective."—The Stage. London.

Royalty, $50—$25

THE SEA HORSE
EDWARD J. MOORE

(Little Theatre) Drama
1 Man, 1 Woman, Interior

It is a play that is, by turns, tender, ribald, funny and suspenseful. Audiences everywhere will take it to their hearts because it is touched with humanity and illuminates with glowing sympathy the complexities of a man-woman relationship. Set in a West Coast waterfront bar, the play is about Harry Bales, a seaman, who, when on shore leave, usually heads for "The Sea Horse," the bar run by Gertrude Blum, the heavy, unsentimental proprietor. Their relationship is purely physical and, as the play begins, they have never confided their private yearnings to each other. But this time Harry has returned with a dream: to buy a charter fishing boat and to have a son by Gertrude. She, in her turn, has made her life one of hard work, by day, and nocturnal love-making; she has encased her heart behind a facade of toughness, utterly devoid of sentimentality, because of a failed marriage. Irwin's play consists in the ritual of "dance" courtship by Harry of Gertrude, as these two outwardly abrasive characters fight, make up, fight again, spin dreams, deflate them, make love and reveal their long locked-up secrets.

ROYALTY, $50-$35

THE AU PAIR MAN
HUGH LEONARD

(Little Theatre) Comedy
1 Man, 1 Woman, Interior

The play concerns a rough Irish bill collector named Hartigan, who becomes a love slave and companion to an English lady named Elizabeth, who lives in a cluttered London town house, which looks more like a museum for a British Empire on which the sun has long set. Even the door bell chimes out the national anthem. Hartigan is immediately conscripted into her service in return for which she agrees to teach him how to be a gentleman rather after the fashion of a reverse Pygmalion. The play is a wild one, and is really the never-ending battle between England and Ireland. Produced to critical acclaim at Lincoln Center's Vivian Beaumont Theatre.

ROYALTY, $50-$35

A Breeze from The Gulf

MART CROWLEY

(Little Theatre) Drama

The author of "The Boys in the Band" takes us on a journey back to a small Mississippi town to watch a 15-year-old boy suffer through adolescence to adulthood and success as a writer. His mother is a frilly southern doll who has nothing to fall back on when her beauty fades. She develops headaches and other physical problems, while the asthmatic son turns to dolls and toys at an age when other boys are turning to sports. The traveling father becomes withdrawn, takes to drink; and mother takes to drugs to kill the pain of the remembrances of things past. She eventually ends in an asylum, and the father in his fumbling way tries to tell the son to live the life he must.

> "The boy is plunged into a world of suffering he didn't create. . . . One of the most electrifying plays I've seen in the past few years . . . Scenes boil and hiss . . . The dialogue goes straight to the heart." Reed, Sunday News.

Royalty, $50–$35

ECHOES

N. RICHARD NASH

(All Groups) Drama
2 Men, 1 Woman, Interior

A young man and woman build a low-keyed paradise of happiness within an asylum, only to have it shattered by the intrusion of the outside world. The two characters search, at times agonizingly to determine the difference between illusion and reality. The effort is lightened at times by moments of shared love and "pretend" games, like decorating Christmas trees that are not really there. The theme of love, vulnerable to the surveillances of the asylum, and the ministrations of the psychiatrist, (a non-speaking part) seems as fragile in the constrained setting as it often is in the outside world.

> ". . . even with the tragic, sombre theme there is a note of hope and possible release and the situations presented specifically also have universal applications to give it strong effect . . . intellectual, but charged with emotion."—Reed.

Royalty, $50–$35

VERONICA'S ROOM

IRA LEVIN

(Little Theatre) Mystery

2 Men, 2 Women, Interior

VERONICA'S ROOM is, in the words of one reviewer, "a chew-up-your-finger-nails thriller-chiller" in which "reality and fantasy are entwined in a totally absorbing spider web of who's-doing-what-to-whom." The heroine of the play is 20-year-old Susan Kerner, a Boston University student who, while dining in a restaurant with Larry Eastwood, a young lawyer, is accosted by a charming elderly Irish couple, Maureen and John Mackey (played on Broadway by Eileen Heckart and Arthur Kennedy). These two are overwhelmed by Susan's almost identical resemblance to Veronica Brabissant, a long-dead daughter of the family for whom they work. Susan and Larry accompany the Mackeys to the Brabissant mansion to see a picture of Veronica, and there, in Veronica's room, which has been preserved as a shrine to her memory, Susan is induced to impersonate Veronica for a few minutes in order to solace the only surviving Brabissant, Veronica's addled sister who lives in the past and believes that Veronica is alive and angry with her. "Just say you're not angry with her," Mrs. Mackey instructs Susan. "It'll be such a blessin' for her!" But once Susan is dressed in Veronica's clothes, and Larry has been escorted downstairs by the Mackeys, Susan finds herself locked in the room and locked in the role of Veronica. Or is she really Veronica, in the year 1935, pretending to be an imaginary Susan?

> The play's twists and turns are, in the words of another critic, "like finding yourself trapped in someone else's nightmare," and "the climax is as jarring as it is surprising." "Neat and elegant thriller."—*Village Voice*.

ROYALTY, $50-$35

MY FAT FRIEND

CHARLES LAURENCE

(Little Theatre) Comedy

3 Men, 1 Woman, Interior

Vicky, who runs a bookshop in Hampstead, is a heavyweight. Inevitably she suffers, good-humouredly enough, the slings and arrows of the two characters who share the flat over the shop; a somewhat glum Scottish youth who works in an au pair capacity, and her lodger, a not-so-young homosexual. When a customer—a handsome bronzed man of thirty—seems attracted to her she resolves she will slim by hook or by crook. Aided by her two friends, hard exercise, diet and a graph, she manages to reduce to a stream-lined version of her former self—only to find that it was her rotundity that attracted the handsome book-buyer in the first place. When, on his return, he finds himself confronted by a sylph his disappointment is only too apparent. The newly slim Vicky is left alone once more, to be consoled (up to a point) by her effeminate lodger.

> "My fat Friend is abundant with laughs."—*Times Newsmagazine*. "If you want to laugh go."—*WCBS-TV*.

ROYALTY, $50-$35

PROMENADE, ALL!
DAVID V. ROBISON

(Little Theatre) Comedy
3 Men, 1 Woman, Interior

Four actors play four successive generations of the same family,
as their business grows from manufacturing buttons to a conglom-
erate of international proportions (in the U.S. their perfume will be
called Belle Nuit; but in Paris, Enchanted Evening). The Broadway
cast included Richard Backus, Anne Jackson, Eli Wallach and Hume
Cronyn. Miss Jackson performed as either mother or grandmother,
as called for; and Cronyn and Wallach alternated as fathers and
grandfathers; with Backus playing all the roles of youth. There are
some excellent cameos to perform, such as the puritanical mother
reading the Bible to her son without realizing the sexual innuendoes;
or the 90-year-old patriarch who is agreeable to trying an experiment
in sexology but is afraid of a heart attack.

> "So likeable; jolly and splendidly performed."—*N.Y. Daily
> News.* "The author has the ability to write amusing lines, and
> there are many of them."—*N.Y. Post.* "Gives strong, lively
> actors a chance for some healthy exercise. And what a time
> they have at it!"—*CBS-TV.*

ROYALTY, $50-$35

ACCOMMODATIONS
NICK HALL

(Little Theatre) Comedy
2 Men, 2 Women, Interior

Lee Schallert, housewife, feeling she may be missing out on something, leaves her husband, Bob, and her suburban home and moves
into a two-room Greenwich Village apartment with two roommates.
One roommate, Pat, is an aspiring actress, never out of characters
or costumes, but, through an agency mix up, the other roommate
is a serious, young, graduate student—male. The ensuing complica-
tions make a hysterical evening.

> "An amusing study of marital and human relations . . . a gem
> . . . It ranks as one of the funniest ever staged."—*Labor Her-
> ald.* "The audience at Limestone Valley Dinner Theater laughed
> at "Accommodations" until it hurt."—*News American.* "Superior
> theater, frivolous, perhaps, but nonetheless superior. It is light
> comedy at its best."—*The Sun, Baltimore.*

ROYALTY, $50-$25

THE GOOD DOCTOR

NEIL SIMON

(All Groups) Comedy
2 Men, 3 Women. Various settings.

With Christopher Plummer in the role of the Writer, we are introduced to a composite of Neil Simon and Anton Chekhov, from whose short stories Simon adapted the capital vignettes of this collection. Frances Sternhagen played, among other parts, that of a harridan who storms a bank and upbraids the manager for his gout and lack of money. A father takes his son to a house where he will be initiated into the mysteries of sex, only to relent at the last moment, and leave the boy more perplexed than ever. In another sketch a crafty seducer goes to work on a wedded woman, only to realize that the woman has been in command the first overture. Let us not forget the classic tale of a man who offers to drown himself for three rubles. The stories are droll, the portraits affectionate, the humor infectious, and the fun unending.

"As smoothly polished a piece of work as we're likely to see all season."—*N.Y. Daily News.* "A great deal of warmth and humor —vaudevillian humor—in his retelling of these Chekhovian tales."—*Newhouse Newspapers.* "There is much fun here . . . Mr. Simon's comic fancy is admirable."—*N.Y. Times.*

(Music available. Write for particulars.)
ROYALTY, $50-$35

The Prisoner of Second Avenue

NEIL SIMON

(All Groups) Comedy
2 Men, 4 Women, Interior

Mel is a well-paid executive of a fancy New York company which has suddenly hit the skids and started to pare the payroll. Anxiety doesn't help; Mel, too, gets the ax. His wife takes a job to tide them over, then she too is sacked. As if this weren't enough, Mel is fighting a losing battle with the very environs of life. Polluted air is killing everything that grows on his terrace; the walls of the high-rise apartment are paper-thin, so that the private lives of a pair of German stewardesses next door are open books to him; the apartment is burgled; and his psychiatrist dies with $23,000 of his money. Mel does the only thing left for him to do: he has a nervous breakdown. It is on recovery that we come to esteem him all the more. For Mel and his wife and people like them have the resilience, the grit to survive.

"Now all this, mind you, is presented primarily in humorous terms."—*N.Y. Daily News.* "A gift for taking a grave subject and, without losing sight of its basic seriousness, treating it with hearty but sympathetic humor . . . A talent for writing a wonderfully funny line . . . full of humor and intelligence . . . Fine fun."—*N.Y. Post.* "Creates an atmosphere of casual cataclysm, and everyday urban purgatory of copelessness from which laughter seems to be released like vapor from the city's manholes."—*Time.*

ROYALTY, $50-$35